Follow *and* Seek

A Guide to Building Joy through Virtue for Teens and Young Adults

Samantha McEnhimer

WESTBOW°
PRESS
A DIVISION OF THOMAS NELSON
& ZONDERVAN

WestBow Press books may be ordered through booksellers or by contacting:

WestBow Press
A Division of Thomas Nelson & Zondervan
1663 Liberty Drive
Bloomington, IN 47403
www.westbowpress.com
1 (866) 928-1240

ISBN: 978-1-4908-8343-4 (sc)
ISBN: 978-1-4908-8344-1 (hc)
ISBN: 978-1-4908-8342-7 (e)

Library of Congress Control Number: 2015909048

Print information available on the last page.

WestBow Press rev. date: 06/04/2015

Say there is anyone thirsty? Come and drink—even if you
have no money! Come, take your choice of wine and milk—it's
all free! Why spend your money on foodstuffs that don't give
you strength? Why pay for groceries that don't do any good?
Listen and I'll tell you where to get good food that fattens
up the soul! Come to me with your ears wide open. Listen,
for the life of your soul is at stake. I am ready to make an
everlasting covenant with you, to give to you all the unfailing
mercies and love that I had for King David. See how I used
him to display my power among the peoples. I made him a
leader among the nations. You also will command nations
you do not know, and peoples unknown to you will come
running to obey, because I, the Lord your God, the Holy
One of Israel, have made you glorious." Seek the Lord while
you can find him. Call on him now while he is near. Let the
wicked change their ways and banish the very thought of doing
wrong. Let them turn to the Lord that he may have mercy on
them. Yes, turn to our God, for he will forgive generously.

—Isaiah 55:1–7

To be glad of life, because it gives you the chance to love and to work and to play and to look up at the stars; to be satisfied with your possessions, but not contented with yourself until you have made the best of them; to despise nothing in the world except falsehood and meanness, and to fear nothing except cowardice; to be governed by your admirations rather than by your disgust; to covet nothing that is your neighbors except his kindness of heart and gentleness of manners; to think seldom of your enemies, and often of your friends, and every day of Christ; and to spend as much time as you can, with body and with spirit, in God's out-of-doors— these are little guideposts on the footpath of peace.[1]

—Henry Van Dyke

Chapter 1

All right, let's begin with the first thing, the thing that caused you to pick up this book and perhaps many others before it. You want to be happy and not say that you are a sad or depressed person. You have moments of gladness just like everyone else—birthdays, anniversaries, etc. But the happiness does not last. You go back to work and the day-to-day drudgery of life, and you forget. You forget how to be happy.

There has to be a better way, right? There has to be a way to be happy all the time, even when the world is crumbling around you. There has to be a way to have joy in spite of the world. If not, what's the point? Well, I agree with you. There is a way. But it is not easy. It requires practice and building virtuous habits. It also requires knowledge of the ways of God and an understanding of righteousness. As we now begin our journey on the path to joy, we must learn a few things so that we understand exactly what it is we are striving for. The first thing we must learn about is what exactly joy is. We can know what joy is by establishing what joy is not.

Joy is not temporary. A true joy—and we will get to the distinction soon—is not subject to circumstance. In fact, as you well know, people can be utterly wealthy with all that they need and more when it comes to worldly possessions, family, and friends and still not appear happy, still not have joy. You know they're unhappy by the negative way they behave and treat others.

Psychology has taught us that there is an underlying cause for all such behaviors. At their core there is fear or anxiety. Not all the time but sometimes we are overwhelmed, tired, or hungry.

1

These three conditions can lead to bad behavior; however, it is temporary, and we often regret what we did or said when we reflect back on our poor behavior. But in general, people behave badly because they are afraid. It may not be obvious, but deep down that is its true ethos. When people are afraid, they cannot also be happy.

On the other hand, people who are relatively poor, who need much and have little, whose circumstances might change for the worse, could very well lose it all and starve to death, and those people may be very happy. They may seem rather upbeat, always nice, always patient, usually smiling and cutting up. We see through these persons that joy is something separate from the circumstances of life.

Now then what exactly is joy, and how is it different from happiness? Bishop Joseph Warren Walker III says that there is a difference between joy and happiness. He believes that happiness is something that happens to you based on the circumstances of your life. Good experiences equal happiness, and bad experiences equal unhappiness. But joy, unlike happiness, does not come and go. Because it is based on revelation, joy is a part of our lives no matter what is happening to us. It is based on our knowledge of things outside of ourselves and our lives on earth. Joy is what allows us to keep hope and peace in the midst of unpleasant circumstances. We may not be happy, but we can and should still have joy. Joy is set apart from happiness in that it has permanence. So for the purposes of this work, we will be looking at what it is that creates joy in a person's life and how we can create this joy for ourselves.

The answer can be found in the works of one of the oldest philosophers of the Western world: Aristotle. In the *Nicomachean Ethics*, Aristotle tells us that happiness comes from having a virtuous character. (He uses the word happiness where we will use joy and the word pleasure where we will use happiness.) It is "a result of virtue and some process of learning or training, to be among the most godlike things; for that which is the prize and end of virtue seems to be the best thing in the world, and something godlike and blessed."[2]

Aristotle is saying quite a lot in this statement, so let us break it down to better understand. First he is saying that happiness (joy) is a result of virtue. This tells us that virtue must be obtained in order to have joy. What then is virtue? It is defined as moral excellence, goodness, righteousness, and conformity of one's life to moral and ethical principles. So if we want to have joy, we must first *conform our lives to certain principles.*

Well then, now that we know we must conform to principles, the next logical question is which principles are the *certain* ones we must conform to? Aristotle also tells us in the previous quote that humans are driven by their desire to be "like God." If this is true, then we must examine what we know about God so that we can discover the principles that lead to virtue and ultimately to joy.

One thing we do know for certain as Christians is that God is good all the time, not some of the time, not when it is convenient, not when God feels like it, and not in response to circumstances. God is good all the time. No matter what. Which makes perfect sense, as God is the one who *gave us* our knowledge of right and wrong. How can we, who are the created, judge the Creator on what is right and what is wrong? If we want to be "like God"— and we must if we want to have joy—then like God, we must be good all the time.

Though God's goodness is clear and undisputable, we may still have a hard time deciding what it means to be good in our own lives. Christ directs us in Luke 18:19–22 when he is approached by a certain ruler who calls him "good master" and asks what he must do to inherit eternal life. Christ responds to this by questioning his use of the word *good.*

> "Why do you call me good?" Jesus asked him.
> "Only God is truly good. But to answer your

> question, you know the commandments: 'You
> must not commit adultery. You must not murder.
> You must not steal. You must not testify falsely.
> Honor your father and mother.'" The man replied,
> "I've obeyed all these commandments since I was
> young." When Jesus heard his answer, he said,
> "There is still one thing you haven't done. Sell all
> your possessions and give the money to the poor,
> and you will have treasure in heaven. Then come,
> follow me.

First Christ rebukes him for using the word *good*, which lets us know that true goodness will never be obtained by us as humans. We were born into sin, and we will never be good in the sense that God is good. This is why we can only hope to be godlike and should never expect to be God. Secondly Jesus lists the things that we must remove from our lives. These sins that Christ lists are keeping us from virtue and are a hindrance to our pursuit of joy. Finally Jesus gives the true path to virtue and joy when he says, "Come, follow me." As we shall see, following Christ is the key to virtue.

The next thing Aristotle tells us is that having joy requires a process of learning and training. This too may seem peculiar to some. You have to train to have joy? Well of course. As we have said, happiness and joy are two different things. Happiness comes as a result of circumstances whereas this joy that we desire is a constant despite circumstance. It is a state of being joyful. Joy requires practice and creating virtuous habits. Just like faith, it has to be built up. So then our next question ought to be this: How do we build up virtuous habits?

Aristotle tells us that habits of virtue are easier learned in childhood, and yet they should be the goal of every adult, for they are obtainable no matter what your age is. In this text we will attempt to gain the knowledge and understanding necessary to have virtuous characters and thus joy impenetrable. We must *learn* how to behave virtuously, or more specifically we must determine what Christ, who is our model for how to live, would do if he were in our shoes. Once we learn what the proper actions are through study, prayer, and obedience to the Holy Spirit, we can *train* ourselves to take those virtuous actions in every moment of our lives. We are creating habits of virtue.

We must remember that we are practicing. We are learning, and we will not be virtuous overnight. Just as "men become builders by building and lyre players by playing the lyre; so too we become just by doing just acts, temperate by doing temperate acts, brave by doing brave acts"[3]. You may very well say that practice makes perfect, and in our case perfection is what we are striving for. The idea of being perfect may be a hard thing for you to imagine. But if you cop out and don't believe that you can be perfect, then surely you have no chance. Christ said to us, "Be ye therefore perfect, even as your father which is in heaven is perfect" (Matthew 5:48 KJV). If we are Christians, if we believe that Christ is the one and only perfect Son of our heavenly Father, then we should not take his words in vain. Remember that joy for us as humans comes from being "like God."

Let us explore more deeply what it means to be "like God." Aristotle tells us that having a virtuous character is among the most godlike things. This seems to make sense, for how many options do we as humans—who are foul, selfish, little beings and go around killing and abusing one another—have to behave like God? Let us see. When we create, we are godlike. God is the ultimate Creator, and whenever we create anything, a song, a story, a mud pie, we do it in his shadow. When we love, we are godlike. God is love in its purest form. As Paul tells us in his first letter to the people of Corinth, love "beareth all things, believeth all things, hopeth all things, endureth all things" (1 Corinthians 13:7 KJV). These words from Paul truly get at the heart of God. God forgives all our sin and still works things together for our good.

So these are the options for us as humans to behave godlike. We can create. We can love, and we can be virtuous. God is Creator. God is love, and God is good. Aristotle believes that of these options—having a virtuous character or being good—leads to the best course for us as humans. In fact, he says that it is the best thing in the world. Though it may not be easy and though it may take a lifetime to achieve, virtue seems to be the purpose for which our lives are created. Developing the habit of virtue is what Paul speaks of when he says he is pressing toward the mark. The high calling of modeling one's self after Christ Jesus, who is God's blueprint for how we should live on this earth, comes with a prize. The prize is joy. Joy is self-sufficient, and it is the most godlike thing. Joy is what allowed Paul and Silas to praise God while they are locked in a dungeon. Joy impenetrable is our goal. Achieving it is what gives our lives meaning and purpose.

Joy is a side effect of being in constant communion with God. This kind of close connection to God is only possible when we behave virtuously like Christ. When we sin, our sin separates us from God, who is without sin, not just because it is wrong but also because when we do things that are opposed to our spiritual nature, which is godlike and without sin, they plague us. Thoughts of our sin consume us. You know what I mean? Think of a time when you have done something you felt you probably should not have done but didn't want to admit as wrong. You can't stop thinking about it either. But why should you think about it. After all, it was such a little thing. Yeah, you were a little bit short with the last customer, but you were busy and stressed out. Or maybe you didn't let that person in at the intersection. You had been in line at the intersection for minutes, and they had just pulled up. For some reason it is these little things that keep popping up in our minds.

The problem here is that when you are thinking about little things, small infractions, you are not thinking about God, who is a huge thing. In those moments, you allow yourself to be separated from God by your sin. That is why a virtuous character is so important. There is no excuse for wrong doing, even something small. Because the small things you do wrong to others and in secret separate you from the presence of God. Nothing in this world is worth that kind of separation.

In future chapters we will probe more deeply into the effects of sin, but I will give you a tip now for what to do when you are consumed with the thoughts of a small infraction. As soon as you realize that you keep thinking about the same little thing, admit that you were wrong. Though it was a small thing, you were not justified in doing it. Ask God to forgive you. Ask God to help you remember this moment so that you will not repeat it. Thank God for grace and mercy and move back into the holy presence. Sing your favorite hymn to yourself, or if you are free to do it, read the Bible. I suggest the Sermon on the Mount (Matthew 5–7). The important thing is to get your eyes back on the prize.

I hope that I have established in your mind that joy should be your life's goal, that it is obtained by being like God, which means having a virtuous character, and that it *is* obtainable. Remember: joy comes from having a virtuous character, it is "a result of virtue and some process of learning or training, to be among the most godlike things; for that which is the prize and end of virtue seems to be the best thing in the world, and something godlike and blessed."[3]

Christ exhorts us to be perfect, and by his perfect example, he directs us on how to do so. As we continue breaking down what it is about virtue that gives us joy and how to obtain that joy, I encourage you to write down quotes and take notes to refer back to as you create a plan for achieving joy. I also recommend that you find a good book on the life of Jesus Christ and diligently study it. Christ is the most godlike person to have ever walked this earth. He lived his life in purpose, and he will be our guide as we journey on the straight and narrow road toward joy.

Never confuse activity with productivity. You can be busy without a purpose, but what's the point?[1]

—Rick Warren

Chapter 2

In our last chapter, we talked about how a virtuous life is godlike and how it leads to joy. In this chapter we will discuss why that is the case. Why does living virtuously work to give you joy? The answer is that the pursuit of virtue gives your life purpose. Google defines purpose as "the reason for which something is done or created or for which something exists." As Christians, we are told that everything in this world has a purpose. This knowledge assures us that there is an answer to the question why are we here. Our God-given purpose is the reason for our existence. Without God, all our actions are meaningless, as we will soon be dead and nothing we do here on earth can change that. We only exist because God wills it so.

If we believe that God created everything and does everything with a purpose, then we must believe that we ourselves also have purpose. As a Christian, you must believe that you were not created by accident and that your life on earth has meaning. That meaning is found in your life's purpose. Just as a tool—let us say a screwdriver—has an intended use, so do you as a human, a creation of God. The screwdriver is used to drive screws. That is the reason it was created, and when you are using it to drive screws, you are helping it to fulfill its purpose. If a screwdriver could feel, I imagine that it would be quite happy in the moments that it is being used for driving screws. But our poor screwdriver is not always being used to drive screws. Most of the time our screwdriver is just sitting in a drawer, not moving in its purpose. Other times—and this is even worse—our screwdriver is being misused. We use it to open paint cans or fish something out that fell behind the dresser. It is moving, but it is not moving in its purpose. It is not driving screws. It is not being used in the way the manual says it should be.

The screwdriver is the same as us. Sometimes as Christians, we are living in purpose. We are reading our Bibles. We are worshipping God. We are loving our neighbors, but unfortunately most of the time we are not living in purpose. Most of the time we are just existing like the screwdriver waiting in the drawer. When we become consumed by the world and "living" our lives, we are in the drawer. In those times we forget to press toward the mark. We forget to seek first the kingdom of God and his righteousness. We do not seek the things of God because we are so busy living in the world and seeking our own purposes.

Sometimes we don't move in purpose, and it's not even because we are busy. Sometimes the enemy has given us a spirit of laziness. The enemy distracts us with TV, Internet, video games, and other earthly pleasures and convinces us that we deserve to take a break and enjoy these things. He says things like, "You can read your Bible tomorrow. You have worked so hard today," or he says, "You don't have to get up and go to church right now. Your favorite show is coming on, and it is only Bible study." He convinces us that the things of God can be put off until tomorrow while worldly entertainments are what we deserve today. Don't be fooled, my brothers and sisters, for it is a lie. If you spend your time on God, you will be refreshed.

Finally there are those times when we are moving outside of our purpose. We are outside of our purpose in those times when we let our pride and self-centeredness get the best of us. We sometimes lose our tempers, behave selfishly, or do any number of other things that we know are sinful, and we feel bad about doing later. These moments should be avoided at all cost. They separate us from God and keep us from achieving our prize of joy and peace.

For us to have joy, we must be always in our purpose. We must stay in constant communion with God, who *is* our purpose, as we are God's creations. Our shared purpose in God is fulfilled by living virtuous lives in which we are trying every day to be more and more like Christ. We have purpose in God simply because we are God's creation, but we also have specific purposes that God has given us as unique individuals. Think of a chessboard. The purposes of all the pieces on the board are to protect the king. They are all unified in that purpose. But each piece also has a unique purpose and set of moves. A rook cannot move like a knight, and a knight cannot move like a pawn. Each character has its own skill set in the overall purpose of protecting the king. So it is with us as Christians. Each of us is responsible for saving our immortal souls through a relationship with Christ Jesus. Each of us also has a responsibility to do God's holy will. Therein lies our unique purpose, and for us to have joy like our little screwdriver, we must act in that purpose. We can discover what this unique purpose is by simply staying in communion with God. God will reveal to us what our purpose is, give us the tools to move in that purpose, and give us peace and assurance that what we are doing is right, even though it will not always be easy.

Joel Osteen talks about living in purpose in his *Hope for Today Bible*. He says that the trials of life can keep us from living in purpose. Setbacks and disappointments can frustrate us to the point that we give up on the dream God placed inside of us. If we want to take back our purpose, we must be determined to do so. Just like the apostle Paul, we must put our all into pursing our purpose. Joel exhorts us to "make a decision." Living in one's purpose does not happen coincidently, but it is the result of deciding to stay in that purpose. It is the result of being intentional about the actions we take in life. It is another habit that we must create for ourselves. We must remember that the enemy is against our purpose. He will do what he can to thwart it and sidetrack us from our destiny. We must be prepared to fight for our destiny, and we do this through virtue just like the apostle Paul did. Any Christian who is trying to live a life that pleases and honors God must admire the life of Paul. Upon his conversion on the Damascus road, Paul gave his life over to a commission from God. Paul pursued his purpose with a passion, and he did not give up on it even under the threat of death. How was he able to do this? By the joy he found living in his purpose. This is the same joy we can all find by living virtuous lives rooted in the purpose God has given us.[2]

When Paul talks about his purpose in Acts 20:22–24, he makes it clear that living in his purpose is what gives life meaning and makes life worth living. "And now I am bound by the Spirit to go to Jerusalem. I don't know what awaits me, except that the Holy Spirit tells me in city after city that jail and suffering lie ahead. But my life is worth nothing to me unless I use it for finishing the work assigned me by the Lord Jesus—the work of telling others the Good News about the wonderful grace of God." Here we see that Paul continues in the purpose he was given even though he knows it will lead to his suffering and eventual death. We learn throughout the New Testament that Paul endures many perils while he is moving in his purpose. Paul is beaten and arrested many times. On his journey to Rome, he endures imprisonment, house arrest, snakebite, and shipwreck. And yet he never gives up on his mission. In fact, it is during this time that he writes to the churches and encourages them to keep the faith and endure till the end. We never see Paul write, "This is too hard," or, "Why is this happening to me?" Instead, he keeps pressing toward the mark because he has joy even in the midst of all his suffering. He has joy because he knows he is doing what he was created to do. He knows that he is fulfilling his purpose just like our screwdriver when it is driving screws.

The joy here comes from the fact that his life is meaningful, even if it is full of suffering. It is suffering with a purpose. In the end Paul died a martyr for Christ Jesus. After his final trial in Rome, he was beheaded by Emperor Nero. Though it may sound sad and even scary to think of Paul dying in this way, I guarantee you that he had joy up until the very last moment. We are all destined to die, so the fear of death should not be the thing that keeps you from your purpose. In fact, we are told by the philosopher Socrates that death is a blessing. Socrates, like Paul, lived a life full of purpose even without the benefit of knowing Christ or even the name of the almighty creator he believed to exist. Socrates too was put to death by the government. He was tried and sentenced for the crime of corrupting the youth. How easy it would have been for him to just stop. He could have declared, "I am seventy years old, and I am just trying to impart wisdom on the younger generation. But if you people don't appreciate me, I will keep my wisdom to myself," but this is not what he did. Instead, Socrates goes to trial, defends his actions, and joyfully accepts the judgment of the city.

Socrates would not compromise his purpose, even under pain of death. In fact, once the verdict had been reached and Socrates was sentenced to death, he continued to live out his purpose by teaching those around him how to live when one knows one is soon going to die.

> He assesses the penalty at death. So be it. [...] Clearly it should be a penalty I deserve, and what do I deserve to suffer or to pay because I have deliberately not led a quiet life but have neglected what occupies most people: wealth, household affairs, the position of general or public orator or the other offices, the political clubs and factions that exist in the city? I thought myself to honest to survive if I occupied myself with those things. I did not follow that path that would have made me of no use either to you or to myself, but I went to each of you privately and conferred upon him

not to care for any of his belongings before caring that he himself should be as good and as wise as possible, not to care for the cities possessions more than the city itself.[3]

In his last breaths, Socrates is still teaching people to be as good and as wise as possible. He is still fulfilling his purpose. He goes on to convey to us not to fear death, for death, Socrates tells us, "is one of two things." Either death is a "complete lack of perception like a dreamless sleep," or it is a "change from here to another place, and what we are told is true and all who have died are there."[4] Either way, Socrates tells us, it is a blessing. Right up until the end of his life, Socrates had joy, for he was living in his purpose and all his actions were meaningful.

Though Socrates's view of virtue may be slightly different from ours, as we have the benefit of Christ's example, he is still living a life of virtue. He lives a life of purpose and not regret. Now you might think, *That is Socrates and Paul, two great men from history. Of course they have purpose, but not little old me. I am just a normal insignificant person. I have no purpose.* If that is what you are thinking, then you are wrong! I hate to tell people that they are wrong, but in this particular case, *you are.* Not only are you wrong, but you are in essence claiming that God was wasting time by creating you. You are saying that God, who took the time to create you, had no real purpose or plan behind it but just did it to do it. Does that really fit into what you know about God? Have you known God to not have an intricate plan for everything? Look back over your life. Has not all that has happened to you lead you to this point? Haven't both the good and the bad worked together to create the person you now are? I am willing to chance that they have. I am willing to chance that God has had a hand in your life from the beginning. God does not waste time.

If you were worth creating and guiding, then of course you are worth a divine destiny and purpose. God loves you. The thoughts that try to diminish your purpose are from the enemy. The enemy sees your potential like the embers of a small fire and tries to stamp it out. Do not allow this. Fight for your purpose. Fight for your joy. Now if you feel that you do have a purpose but you have yet to put your finger on what it could be, we should talk about spiritual gifts. The Bible speaks about spiritual gifts in multiple places. These gifts come from the Holy Spirit. He is the invisible advocate that lives on the inside of us. Jesus left the Spirit for us on earth when He ascended into heaven. The Holy Spirit does several things for Christians, but for now we will talk mainly about spiritual gifts. In 1 Corinthians 12:7–11, Paul tells us,

> A spiritual gift is given to each of us so we can help each other. To one person the Spirit gives the ability to give wise advice; to another the same Spirit gives a message of special knowledge. The same Spirit gives great faith to another, and to someone else the one Spirit gives the gift of healing. He gives one person the power to perform miracles, and another the ability to prophesy. He gives someone else the ability to discern whether a message is from the Spirit of God or from another spirit. Still another person is given the ability to speak in unknown languages, while another is given the ability to interpret what is being said. It is the one and only Spirit who distributes all these gifts. He alone decides which gift each person should have.

All these spiritual gifts are in the world and are necessary for the body of Christ. These are all gifts given to us by the Holy Spirit. One or more of these may be gifts that you possess. In order to learn more about the gifts, I suggest you read 1 Corinthians 12–14. Another place Paul talks about gifts is in Romans 12:6–8,

In his grace, God has given us different gifts for doing certain things well. So if God has given you the ability to prophesy, speak out with as much faith as God has given you. If your gift is serving others, serve them well. If you are a teacher, teach well. If your gift is to encourage others, be encouraging. If it is giving, give generously. If God has given you leadership ability, take the responsibility seriously. And if you have a gift for showing kindness to others, do it gladly.

As you read this passage, you will be drawn to one or more of these gifts over the others. This is the first step in living out your purpose and running your unique race. As you pray and meditate, think about the gift that is yours. Ask God to reveal to you his plan for your gift. Really listen for the answer. Look for it in your interactions with others. Be open to new opportunities in your church or community, but be cautious. Do not rush into things, but judge things by their fruit. As you begin discerning God's plan for your life, do not allow the activities of that plan to become more important than your relationship with God.

Purpose is wonderful and moving in our purpose can give our lives meaning and joy. But being in constant communion with God is our true purpose; it gives our true meaning. Our relationship with God must always be the first and most important thing in our lives. The enemy is clever, and he will try to twist our purpose so we become so busy that we no longer take the time to pray, to meditate, or to study God's Word. This is an easy trap to fall into, but you cannot allow yourself to become ensnared. Remember that this world will soon come to an end, but your relationship with God is everlasting and never-ending. Let the Holy Spirit lead all your actions, and you shall avoid the enemies trap. Now that you know the significance of purpose in your life, I exhort you to pray and meditate on it. Ask God what it is you were put on this earth to do. Read a book that speaks about purpose and fill it with margin comments and highlights. I recommend *The Purpose-Driven Life* by Rick Warren. Regardless of what your purpose is, let the Holy Spirit guide you, and always remember to put God first.

If you love your father or mother more than you love me, you are not worthy of being mine; or if you love your son or daughter more than me, you are not worthy of being mine. If you refuse to take up your cross and follow me, you are not worthy of being mine. If you cling to your life, you will lose it; but if you give up your life for me, you will find it.

—Matthew 10:37–39

Chapter 3

Meaning is what makes life worth living. It is what makes the unbearable ... bearable. It is the driving force behind our decisions and our actions. Another word for it is significance. We all want to be significant in life, maybe not to everyone but to someone. As Christians, we believe that we are significant to God. God loves us and cares for us regardless of our actions. Once we come to realize how much God loves, this realization makes us want to love God back, and loving God makes us want to please God. Thus, pleasing God gives our lives significance and meaning. It becomes the driving force of our decisions and our actions.

In this chapter's opening quote, Jesus is giving instructions to his disciples. He tells them that the worth of their lives can be measured by their love for him as the son of God. He tells them that they will lose their lives if they cling to them but save them if they give them up to him. Christ here is speaking not about losing life in the sense of dying and being laid in one's grave but about the life that one lives daily. The struggle and toil of everyday life can be lost or gained with Christ. Our everyday is what Christ wants us to give him with *his promise* that it will be returned to us in the form of meaning. If we follow Christ's example, stay in constant communion with God, and allow ourselves to be led by the Holy Spirit, we set ourselves up for a meaningful life full of joy. God will order our steps, and though there will be hardships, we can endure them with the knowledge that they are growing us, making us more like God's own son. We must remember that God allowed *his Son* to endure adversities while he was on earth. So we, the followers or disciples of Christ, cannot expect to avoid trials just as our Master did not. We must be crucified with Christ, and like Christ, we must know that there is meaning behind our suffering.

During the 1940s, the world experienced its second world war. The German Army, which was led by the dictator Adolph Hitler, imprisoned, tortured, and massacred the Jewish people of Europe. During this time a Jewish man named Victor Frankl was imprisoned in several Nazi concentration camps, including the infamous Auschwitz. Victor was a psychologist before he entered Nazi imprisonment, but his experience during the three years in the camps made him significant. During his time of horror at the hands of the Nazis, Dr. Frankl came to a deep understanding of suffering and the meaning behind it. He came out of the camps spiritually stronger with his faith intact and ready to pen multiple books on man's search for meaning in life. In his book *Man's Search for Meaning*, Frankl tells us that "man's main concern is not to gain pleasure or to avoid pain but rather to see a meaning in his life."[1] He explains that finding meaning in our lives is the driving force behind most of our actions. When we do not feel that our lives have meaning, we can slip into what is called the existential vacuum.

The term existential vacuum simply describes a void of meaning or purpose that results in certain types of behavior. Frankl tells us that because man no longer has to work constantly in order to ensure survival and is no longer in the position of being born into the occupation of his parents, he now has too many options. It used to be that we had to hunt and gather all day in order to provide ourselves with food, clothing, and shelter. Then we got into agriculture, and we still had to work very hard on our farms. This kind of life, though it was difficult, was meaningful. We saw the fruits of our labor. During the industrial age, this was taken away from us. Jobs became departmentalized, and we no longer saw the fruits of our labor. But there was no question as to what you would do when you grew up. You would work in the same place your parents worked. Now, however, we have freedom. We Americans no longer have a given path that we are obligated to follow. We are like the everyman that Frankl talks about in his book. We do not have a designated function in life either from tradition or from our own desire. The options are so unlimited that making a choice has become overwhelming.

The epidemic that is plaguing America's youth today *is boredom* and a lack of meaning. This is why teen pregnancy and substance abuse are at an all-time high. The youth are trying to fill the vacuum of meaninglessness with babies, drugs, and alcohol. As computers and robots take away more and more jobs that were previously held by humans, average people find themselves with an abundance of leisure time. As Christians, we know that too much leisure time can be dangerous. Too much free time positions us to be swayed by the enemy. Things we would not normally have thought to do become reasonable when we are bored. Normally you might not have spent the entire afternoon watching YouTube videos, but you were bored. You had nothing better to do, and as we have said before, the enemy convinced you that you deserved a break. Or perhaps you had too much of something you shouldn't have had because you had no reason not to. It could have been too much to drink or too much ice cream. Why not after all? You didn't have a reason to stay sober or a reason to stay thin. If it was just the one time, it might not be a problem. The problem comes in when the enemy sees our weakness and exploits it, making it a habit.

Meaning is what gives you a reason to do certain things and not to do other things. The problem for us may be that we have not grasped the meaning of our individual lives. Once we establish the meaning of our lives, we are able to make decisions based on that meaning. Just like our purpose and our joy, God gives our lives meaning. If there were no God of any kind, there would be no point in doing anything. It would all just be wasted time until we die and go into nothingness. But since there is a God, our lives as humans have meaning. Because our God is good, we have meaning as individuals as well.

In our struggle to be like Christ and our push toward a relationship with God, tension arises in our lives. God gives us tension in the form of tests and challenges to stretch and grow us, thereby giving our lives meaning. Frankl tells us that people need tension in their lives. People need goals and turmoil that tries to frustrate those goals in order to find purpose and meaning in life. We are happiest when we have a significant purpose to struggle for. By reading this and choosing to develop virtuous habits that will lead to your ultimate joy, you are creating meaning for yourself, but you are also creating struggle and tension. Training yourself mentally, physically, or spiritually always requires struggle and sacrifice, but it is a meaningful and worthwhile struggle.

Your life's significance is found in your service to God. Again, as Frankl tells us, our humanity is unearthed when we are transcending ourselves. We must be fully immersed in a cause or another person in order to forget ourselves. When we do that, we actualize our humanity. Actualization only happens when we forget about ourselves and live for Christ and for others. The fact is that God has created us in such a way that we are happiest when we are doing for others. A man or woman might work themselves to the bone for the love of their children. If there was no child, there would be no meaning in such work. By loving their child, they have meaning in their lives, meaning to endure things they do not enjoy. Others find meaning in their work. They fulfill purpose in what they do, and for them, meaning is achieved in giving themselves over to their noble profession. Many artists experience meaning in this way as well. Some artists divulge their souls in their work. They find meaning and purpose in what they create.

As Christians, doing for others can be perceived as a selfish act because of the joy and the sense of peace we receive when we do so. This is true for all humans. When we do for others, we move in our purpose, and we are rewarded by God with a feeling of joy. When we step out of ourselves and open up to God's plan for our lives, the existential vacuum is demolished by the meaning and purpose God fills us with. If we focus on getting meaning out of life by doing for others instead of thinking only of ourselves, we can avoid the regret that comes with a day wasted and mistakes made.

Now there are times when we are tired or irritated, and we feel justified in not giving our all. But of course, we later regret that choice because the actions we choose to take *instead* are not meaningful. Even when we are exhausted, we will find more joy in doing meaningful things than we will in giving ourselves an excuse to be lazy. You must remember that we do not fight against flesh and blood but against powers and principalities. The fight over our flesh must take place in our minds with the assistance of the Holy Spirit. Spirit and mind must come together to fight against the flesh. I am not saying that you should never have a break. But your breaks should be just that—breaks, pauses between vigorous periods of meaningful effort. And your breaks should be filled with planned rest and entertainment, *not idle time.*

In conclusion, we should seek to find meaning in all our actions, even those that we did not choose and that might cause us pain. Meaning comes from doing things that are outside of ourselves and giving ourselves to others just as Christ did. Everything that Jesus does is meaningful even and especially when he was crucified. In order to have joy, we must choose meaningful actions as often as possible. The enemy will do his best to convince us to be lazy and selfish. We must fight him on this. We must fight for our purpose, our meaning, and our joy. As for me, I have come to love the feeling of being exhausted when I go to bed. I sleep peacefully with the knowledge that I have been productive that day and that I have given my time to my fellow man and to my God. On those days, I have no regrets. My life is meaningful, purposeful, and joyful. As you explore the meaning in your own life, I highly recommend you read *Man's Search for Meaning* by Victor Frankl. I know it will be as much a blessing to your life as it has been to mine.

Let there be tears for what you have done. Let there be sorrow and deep grief. Let there be sadness instead of laughter, and gloom instead of joy. Humble yourselves before the Lord, and he will lift you up in honor.

—James 4:9–10

Chapter 4

Suffering is a part of our lives. No matter who you are or how righteous you think you are, you are sure to experience suffering at several points during your life here on earth. Your suffering is a part of God's plan for your life. Some think it strange that Christians, disciples of Christ, and children of God should have to suffer. These people believe that a relationship with God should come with the perk of being free from suffering and pain. But why would one think that? All you have to do is look at the suffering of Christ to see that a relationship with God does not equal freedom from suffering. If we are going to be disciples of Christ, we must share in our Master's affliction.

Suffering, we know, is not all bad. We use suffering to teach both children and adults and to correct inappropriate behavior. Children receive spankings or other types of punishment to correct their behavior. As older and wiser adults, we inflict suffering on them to teach them that there are consequences for their actions. We allow them to experience a little bit of pain now in the hopes that it will save them from a great deal of pain in the future. If a child reaches for a hot pot, you might pop his or her hand and inflict pain and suffering on the kid, but you do this because you know that if the child ever does touch the hot pot, the suffering he or she will then experience will be far greater than the light pop you inflicted. You correct a child's behavior in order to save them from a greater future pain. As a society, we do the same with criminals. We lock them up and demand that they suffer the loss of their freedom in order to teach them a lesson. Thus, we see that even people inflict intentional suffering on one another in order to benefit other people.

In fact, as adults, we are often grateful for the corrective suffering inflicted on us as children. The lessons we learned as children taught us how to behave in society. We all know how obnoxious it is when you run into an adult who has poor manners, people who are loud in a movie theater, who won't hold the door for you, or who can't say please and thank you. We often think to ourselves, *Who raised you, and why did they not teach you better?* If we as humans can derive a benefit from suffering, just think how much more God can do with it. Suffering is used by God in many ways. It is used to correct behavior, to help us grow, to connect us to one another through compassion, to test our faith, and to give our lives meaning.

God uses suffering to correct our behavior just as we correct the behavior of children. When we sin, we separate ourselves from God. But over time we can become accustomed to our sin, and with the assistance of the enemy, we can become convinced that what we are doing is not sinful. We justify our sin. When this happens, God needs to punish us in order to correct the sinful behavior. For example, you may be a person who drinks and drives. You might have gotten away with it for a long time with no DUIs or accidents. But if you continue in this behavior, at some point God is likely to punish you in an attempt to get you to stop. You could receive a DUI and lose lots of money and privileges. Or you could have an accident and be physically injured. Or maybe you hit some person and kill them. Not only may there be jail time, but now you must live with the knowledge that you've ended another person's life. Any of these three options would lead to your suffering. Whatever the punishment, the crime was against God, and the punishment was inflicted by God. God allowed the suffering. That is why Peter tells us in 1 Peter 3:16–17, "Keep your conscience clear. Then if people speak against you, they will be ashamed when they see what a good life you live because you belong to Christ. Remember: it is better to suffer for doing good, if that is what God wants, than to suffer for doing wrong." Here Peter states quite clearly that we as Christians will suffer, and he implores us to only do good so that we will at least have the benefit of a clear conscious; however, he also makes it unmistakable that we will still suffer even when we are doing good.

Sometimes God needs to remove us from certain people or places so that we can grow and discover our destinies. We have to be pushed out of our comfort zones sometimes. Just like a mother bird pushes her chicks out of the nest when it is time for them to fly, God pushes us out of our places of security so that we can encounter new places and new people. The experience for us can be a terrifying one just like it can be for the baby birds. As human animals, we enjoy sameness and comfort, and we are often fearful of change. We are not always eager to get into the new season God has prepared for us. Many times the people we are around are keeping us stagnant. In those times, we see a once happy and pleasant relationship suddenly start falling apart. Out of nowhere the problems cannot be fixed, and your heart is left broken. You don't know what you did to make the other person suddenly begin treating you so badly. Those are the times when God is pushing us out of the nest. Sometimes we have trouble on our jobs. People may lie about you or make the workplace so unbearable that you are either fired or forced to quit. Often these situations arise because God has something better for us, though in the moment we cannot see it. As Christians, we must know that we will get the victory at the end of our suffering. In the end we will be able to look back and say it was for our good that the job or relationship came to an end.

The Bible gives us a clear example of suffering with a purpose in the life of Joseph. God gave him great dreams and a great anointing, but his anointing sparked jealousy in the hearts of his older brothers. Their jealousy led to Joseph being sold into slavery, being imprisoned, and experiencing a great deal of suffering.

However, it also led to the rescue of Egypt, the salvation of his family, and Joseph's great title and position. If Joseph had not endured so much suffering, he would not have achieved the destiny God had for his life. When he confronted his brothers, Joseph said to them, "Don't be afraid of me. Am I God, that I can punish you? You intended to harm me, but God intended it all for good. He brought me to this position so I could save the lives of many people. No, don't be afraid. I will continue to take care of you and your children" (Genesis 50:19–21). Joseph acknowledged that his suffering had a purpose, and he forgave his brothers their hand in it.

Joseph's suffering not only stretched him and moved him to where God wanted him to be but also gave him a testimony. Suffering always blesses us by giving us a testimony that allows us to connect to others who have similar experiences. If you never suffered, how could you sympathize with someone who is suffering? As a child, I remember picking on those children whose parents didn't believe in spankings. If you never got hit, you couldn't have a story about it. The current Dalai Lama believes that suffering connects all people to one another. It is one element of life that we all share and cannot avoid. When we experience suffering, we are sharing this common fate with humans all over the world. Just as we all eat and sleep, we all experience suffering. Remembering past suffering gives us compassion for those around us who are currently suffering.[1]

Compassion for others is a side effect of our suffering. Our suffering gives us a basis for understanding the problems and sufferings of others. We need compassion in order to follow Christ's mandate that we love our neighbors as ourselves. Having compassion for our neighbors' suffering, which mirrors our own past or current suffering, helps us show the love of Christ. Therefore, suffering brings us closer both to our fellow man and to our God.

We know that suffering is a God-sanctioned part of human existence because even Christ was called to suffer. Jesus, however, did not experience it for any of the reasons we have discussed. He had not sinned, so there was no need for punishment. He had no need of stretching, as he was God in human form. He had no need to learn compassion, as he was naturally compassionate to mankind's suffering. That is why he volunteered to be sacrificed for our sins. Christ suffered for his faith. Jesus suffered to show the world that no matter what happened, he would trust God and be obedient.

Another example of suffering for faith can be found in Job. As we know from the book of Job, God allowed Satan to attack Job in several areas. God even invited Satan to do so. Job went through immense suffering as a testament to his unwavering trust in God. He had enough sense to know that he was God's creation, not his own. His body and his life belonged to God. Though Job, unlike Christ, did not know why he was suffering, he did not lose faith. In the end Job is rewarded for enduring his test with a double portion of what he lost. Through the lives of Job and Jesus, we see that oftentimes suffering comes as a test of our faith. Though it is painful when we are in the valley, once we reach the mountaintop, we can look back and say that it has been worth the suffering. The suffering endured as a test of our faith is meaningful. It is a part of our purpose, and it is working in our favor.

When we suffer, we are given acute focus. It is very difficult for us to think of anything outside of our own suffering. Our suffering fills our lives like air in a balloon. Think of yourself as a balloon with no air in it. When pressure is applied, you stretch and change. If a balloon had feelings, I imagine that being blown up would be rather painful for it, but when the stretching is complete, the balloon is better. Now it can float into the air. If the right gas was added, it could float right up to heaven. It had to endure a painful process to get there, but the balloon is now living out its purpose. And now it is closer to God. When God

31

fills us and stretches us, we are made more godlike. Like the balloon, we can float a little bit higher until one day we can float right up to heaven.

I hope this chapter has helped you to see that suffering is a part of your life and is no cause to lose your joy. Once you accept the fact that you will suffer here on earth, you can begin looking for one of the causes behind your times of suffering. Even if you cannot determine the reason, you can be confident that there is one, that this moment of suffering is a part of God's plan for your life, and that *it is* for your good. Do not let it steal your joy. Keep trusting God, stand on his Word, and remember that the sufferings of this world are only for a moment and that you have everlasting life as your reward when you complete your race. As I close this chapter, I exhort you not to read a book but to write one. Think back over your life and your times of suffering. Write them down, and write down how God ended the suffering. What was its purpose? What came out of it? What will you learn from it? Remember that you are on earth simply to do God's holy will and save your immortal soul. How has suffering contributed to your purpose?

Don't you realize that in a race everyone runs, but only one person gets the prize? So run to win! All athletes are disciplined in their training. They do it to win a prize that will fade away, but we do it for an eternal prize. So I run with purpose in every step. I am not just shadowboxing. I discipline my body like an athlete, training it to do what it should. Otherwise, I fear that after preaching to others I myself might be disqualified.

—1 Corinthians 9:24–27

Chapter 5

In chapter 2, we touched on running your race, and we discussed how God gives us each a unique and personal purpose for our lives. In this chapter, we will analogize personal purpose to a runner racing toward the finish. We will discuss what it means and what is required to run our races. Our lives as Christians can be compared to races because we, like runners, have a goal to reach. The goal we reach toward is the kingdom of God both in our afterlives and here on earth. Here on earth, our goal is to develop the kingdom of God by living in our unique purpose, which leads to God's order on earth and our impenetrable joy. In order to have joy, we must take the advice of Paul. If we do as Paul exhorts us in the opening quote and look at our lives as a race that we desire to win, then we are going to need to know how to run in order to be successful. When athletes are preparing to race, they learn how to breathe, when to jog as opposed to sprint, and how to hold their bodies for optimal wind resistance. In order to be the best, the athlete needs quite a bit of preparation. If our goal is to win, then we too must prepare and practice before the race.

In order to win your race, you need three things. You need perseverance, obedience, and love. An athlete needs these same three things in a race. She needs perseverance to endure all the rigors and hardships of training. She needs obedience to her coach in order to be her best and work optimally at her sport. She may not agree with all of the coach's decisions, but trust and obedience are a necessary part of her training. Finally she needs a love of the sport. If she did not love it, she would not be able to endure the severities of training and obedience. If she did not love it, she would quit. She would not force her body to do what it should do as opposed to what it wants to do. As Christians, we need these same three things to win our prize of joy. In order to build our virtuous habits, achieve moral excellence, and win first prize, we need these three skills. Let's look at each of them individually and how they apply to our races.

The first is perseverance. Google defines perseverance as "steadfastness in doing something despite difficulty or delay in achieving success." This definition is powerful. By saying we need perseverance to win our race, we are saying outright that there will be delay and difficulty in achieving success. There is no getting around it. Winning your race will not come easy. Creating virtuous habits is not what your flesh is naturally inclined to do. You must fight your flesh, your mind, and unholy spirits on a daily basis. You must persevere through the temptation. As we have said before, your life *will* include suffering. But all suffering has meaning, and oftentimes the meaning is found when you persevere through the suffering. Again the definition says that we are steadfast *despite* difficulty. As we journey toward joy, we will notice a parallel between our journey and perseverance. Where there is one, the other is surely there as well.

A great part of the race you run will call for perseverance. When times are difficult, we Christians should use the Word of God to sustain us and help us to persevere. Joel Osteen tells us to use God's Word to help drive us and give ourselves that perseverance. We must remember that the enemy is watching us and that he will attempt to make things difficult for us because he can see that we are about to fulfill our purpose. This is why perseverance is so key. We may be incredibly close to achieving our purpose, but if we don't see it around the corner, we could be tempted to give up. That is why speaking words of life over ourselves is a necessity. I love how Joel words it. He not only tells us that we should persevere, but he also gives us the tool necessary to persevere, the Word of God. The Word of God is what gives us strength. We all have memories of the times when God has saved us in the past. We all have memories of situations that looked dire, but somehow everything worked out. These promises, given to us by God and found in the *Holy Bible*, are the rocks on which we stand steadfast when we are persevering. Though difficulty will come, we must use the Word of God as a tool to keep us going. In order for us to believe in what God says and what God has done, we must know the Word of God.[1]

Our friend Paul talks about perseverance in his letters to Timothy. Paul says,

> Endure suffering along with me, as a good soldier of Christ Jesus. Soldiers don't get tied up in the affairs of civilian life, for then they cannot please the officer who enlisted them. And athletes cannot win the prize unless they follow the rules. And hardworking farmers should be the first to enjoy the fruit of their labor. Think about what I am saying. The Lord will help you understand all these things. (2 Timothy 2:3–7)

All three of Paul's illustrations bring to mind uncomfortable states of being—being a solider, being an athlete, and being a hardworking farmer. Paul wants us to imagine ourselves in one of these roles, not as an occupation but as a way of life. All three illustrations call for hard work and perseverance, but they also all come with a prize. As we run the individual races for which we were put on this earth, we must have perseverance in order to win.

The next skill we need is obedience. Every professional athlete is going to have a trainer or a coach. There must be someone who is looking at the athlete objectively, someone who knows the sport and can make corrections. No winner can go without a coach. It is the same with us as Christians. The Holy Spirit is our coach. He is inside of us, making corrective commentary. He is doing his best to make us our best. If the athlete does not want to listen to the coach, she will not get first prize. Though she may not always agree just as we do not always agree with the Holy Spirit, she is obedient anyway. She is obedient because she knows that the coach can see the situation better than she can and that he has her best interest at heart. In order for us to be obedient, we must keep our goals in front of us. We must remember the prize for which we race.

There are going to be times when we will not understand the Holy Spirit's commands, and then we will not want to obey them. But we must remember that obedience is the only way to win our race and that winning our race is the only thing worth doing. All else on this earth is temporary and futile. Paul talks about running our race in Hebrews 12:1–2. Paul says,

> Therefore, since we are surrounded by such a huge crowd of witnesses to the life of faith, let us strip off every weight that slows us down, especially the sin that so easily trips us up. And let us run with endurance the race God has set before us. We do this by keeping our eyes on Jesus, the champion who initiates and perfects our faith. Because of the joy awaiting him, he endured the cross, disregarding its shame. Now he is seated in the place of honor beside God's throne.

Paul exhorts us to look unto Jesus for inspiration in running our race. He says that Christ ran his race for the joy that was set before him. Here we confirm that joy is the goal for which we run. We know that Christ prayed to God, hoping to avoid his fate on the cross, but in the end he says, "Not my will but thy will be done," and accepts the last lap of his race. He is obedient to his father's will. We must do the same with our directions from the Holy Spirit. We will not always like it; however, there are rules to running in this Christian race, and they must be followed.

God put in us the desire to be great and Christlike. It is no accident that we all feel that way. Each of us has felt at some point in our lives that we might be "the one." There is nothing wrong with this feeling. It is a good thing, but our greatness must come in God's way. We must be obedient in order to obtain victory. Jesus made this point in his response to his disciples after they came to him and wanted to know who was the greatest among them. Christ said this in response: "Whoever wants to be first must take last place and be the servant of everyone else" (Mark 9:35). Christ illustrates how we ought not to shy away from greatness, just our perception of what it is to be great. It is perfectly acceptable for us to want to be great, but we must also accept that there are rules we must follow in order to achieve our greatness. In order for us to win our race and get first prize, we need obedience to our coach, the Holy Spirit.

The final skill we need is love. In order to persevere and be obedient, we need to love what we are doing, though not necessarily in every moment. After all, there will be moments of disappointment and difficulty, but if we are to persevere through them, we will do it because of love. For example, if you are a parent, at some point your baby is going to get sick, and he or she will throw up all over you. When this happens, do you toss the baby to the side in disgust? No, because you love your baby. If an adult whom you do not love throws up on you, you will probably be quite upset. After all, it's disgusting when someone throws up on you. The difference in these two scenarios is the love. You love your child, so you endure what you would not otherwise endure. The same principle can be applied to the athlete and to us as Christians. When we obey the commands of God and the direction of the Holy Spirit, we will be led to do for others. Remember: God has programmed us to get joy out of helping others. The more we do for others, the more we love it, but we do not come into this love overnight. It takes obedience and perseverance. In his book *Mere Christianity*, C. S. Lewis reveals to us that love for others only comes after we learn to truly love God, and we only learn to truly love God once we have developed a relationship with Him built on trust and obedience. We learn from Lewis that love is a side effect of obedience. The more obedient we are, the more we see God's purpose for our lives. The vision and experience of our purpose is what grows our love for God. When we see how much God loves us, we cannot help but love God back.[2]

Second Peter 1:5–8 brings up another interesting aspect of love and its part in running our races. Peter says,

> In view of all this, make every effort to respond to God's promises. Supplement your faith with a generous provision of moral excellence, and moral excellence with knowledge, and knowledge with self-control, and self-control with patient endurance, and patient endurance with godliness, and godliness with brotherly affection, and brotherly affection with love for everyone. The more you grow like this, the more productive and useful you will be in your knowledge of our Lord Jesus Christ.

Peter highlights how we need both a love for God and also a love for people. God loves people more than they can love themselves. If we want to show God our love, we must do it by loving what God loves. When we do that, we become fruitful and useful by bringing more people to a relationship with God. Even if it is not obvious, all our actions have consequences. Though it may seem that the people we helped are not appreciative of what we did for them, we can rest soundly knowing that we did the right thing and that our actions are chipping away at the sin holding those people hostage. When we do for others as instructed by the Holy Spirit, we help bring the kingdom of God on earth.

I hope this chapter has made the phrase "running your race" clearer to you. I hope that you understand how it is that a Christian runs a race, what prize a Christian runs for, and what is required of a Christian in the race. In order to win our races, we must have perseverance to get through difficulty, obedience to the Holy Spirit, and love for both God and other people. God's purpose for our lives will always have something to do with showing Christian love to others. The book recommendation for this chapter is *I Have a Dream: Writings and Speeches that Changed the World*. In Dr. King, we see a recent and powerful example of a man running his race. King perseveres through much difficulty. He is obedient to the commands of the Holy Spirit by staying nonviolent, and he love's God by loving his neighbor and serving them both in a fight for justice and equality. Dr. King gives us an excellent example, and I highly recommend reading his works.

When a man finds that it is his destiny to suffer, he will have to accept his suffering as his task; his single and unique task. He will have to acknowledge the fact that even in suffering he is unique and alone in the universe.[1]

—Victor Frankl

Chapter 6

Now that we have talked about running our race and the skills we need to do it, we must also look at the parts of our destiny that help bring us to our goal but are also disagreeable to us. We call these bumps in the road trials. Once we come into a relationship with Christ, we begin running the race. We begin the training, and day by day we grow closer to the finish line. Outside of the race, God also works on our behalf by providing us with challenges. Opportunities to run up hill strengthen our bodies and make us better able to run on a flat plane. Thus, God provides us with the trials that strengthen us and make us tougher and more godly. We touched on this when we talked about suffering. We said that God uses suffering to stretch us. The trials and the process are God's ways of preparing us and training us.

Nobody wants to learn through trials. We would all rather be taught the lesson in a more indirect way. The Bible is there to teach us, but of course, like schoolchildren, we don't study if there is no test coming up. Without diligent study and practice, we do not learn the lesson. Thus, we are obliged to learn through experience, though we do not want to. We learn lessons faster and with longer lasting results through experience than we ever did with schoolbooks. Just like a child touching a hot stove, we learn from painful experience, and we do not forget what we learned. How can you truly know in your soul that you can trust God unless you have been down to nothing and have experienced God's ability to care for you? It is all well and good to read a Bible story about how

God took care of Elijah, but you don't really internalize the lesson until you share in Elijah's experience of having nothing. Though the lesson may be painful, it is memorable, and your faith will have grown from the trial. Besides that, oftentimes God has tried to teach us subtlety, but to no avail. We may have had an uneasy feeling, or a friend may have given us some advice. These are both warnings from God, but the lesson doesn't really stick until we are caught and punished. Some lessons you may learn without the need for a trial. After all, some children listen and never get near the hot stove. Everyone is unique, and no two people will go through the exact same trials. But everyone does need correction. Instead of touching the hot stove, you may find something else to get into, like the power socket. The point is that everyone needs to go through trials, though everyone does not need to be taught the same things necessarily. The trials we endure are the process through which God teaches these lessons and strengthens us for the next leg of our race.

On the topic of trials, James, the brother of Jesus and leader of the early church in Jerusalem, in the first chapter of his book tells us, "Dear brothers and sisters, when troubles of any kind come your way, consider it an opportunity for great joy. For you know that when your faith is tested, your endurance has a chance to grow. So let it grow, for when your endurance is fully developed, you will be perfect and complete, needing nothing" (James 1:2–4). James exhorts us to accept the process, to embrace the difficulties rather than fight them, remembering that they are helping us grow. This passage fits in perfectly with our goal of obtaining joy through virtue, and I agree with James that we should not fight the process; however, I also believe in preventative measures. I like the idea of taking a proactive role and learning the necessary lessons without too much suffering. But the problem, of course, is in my flawed humanity. It takes a lot of dedication and perseverance on my part to behave morally all the time. And even if I do live a righteous life, like Job, I may still find myself suffering. So I come back around to what James has said and accept my suffering and look for the blessing in it.

So now that I have accepted that suffering and trials are a part of my life and a part of the process I must go through to reach my goal, what then do I do? I like what C. S. Lewis has to say on the subject. Lewis tells us that we must learn to forgive ourselves when we make mistakes and cause our own suffering, and we must learn to get back out there and try again. Too often people give up after they experience suffering because they feel like failures. But this is not the case at all. What is really happening is that we are being trained to try again. Also we are learning to rely completely on God and to stop looking to ourselves. This lesson cannot be learned overnight, so we continue to endure suffering until we understand that God is the only source for wisdom in every situation. Again, we know that perfection is the goal for our lives and that we will make mistakes. Since it is inevitable that we will error, the failure is not in the error itself. The only failure comes when we give up on our goal, when we stop. As long as we are determined to persevere through our trials, then the trials will do what they were intended to do, which is stretch and grow us.[2]

I am sure I do not have to tell you that muscles are created by the tearing and rebuilding of tissue. I am sure I do not have to tell you about the pressure that coal endures in order to create a precious diamond. Evidence for the need to endure a painful process in order to create something valuable is everywhere in nature. We need simply look around us to know that we are not alone in our trials and that they are parts of God's plan. Just because we have pain does not mean God has abandoned us. Paul comforts us in Romans 8:35–37, which says,

> Can anything ever separate us from Christ's love? Does it mean he no longer loves us if we have trouble or calamity, or are persecuted, or hungry, or destitute, or in danger, or threatened

with death?(As the Scriptures say, "For your sake we are killed every day; we are being slaughtered like sheep.") No, despite all these things, overwhelming victory is ours through Christ, who loved us.

We must remember our prize and our victory as we go through the process. Our trials are but for a moment in comparison to the eternity we will spend with God. We must remember that heaven is prepared as a reward for the trials we endured. If we want the reward, we must put in the work.

Finally as I wrap up this chapter, I'll leave those of you who like to prepare for the test with the words of C. S. Lewis. Lewis reminds us that it is paramount that we begin our day in prayer and meditation. The first temptation of every day happens immediately when we awake and the worries and concerns of the day bombard us. Before we enter the world and all its chaos, we must spend that valuable time in the morning reconnecting with the Lord and getting ourselves out of the way so that we can be used by him. If you can quiet yourself, die to the things of the flesh, and tap into the Holy Spirit, you will be better prepared than most when the inevitable trials come. Do not think about how they are inconveniencing you, but instead think of what God wants from this situation. Why is this happening, and what are you supposed to do? Pray and truly listen for God's answer as you live out your day. As always, trust in the Lord with all thine heart and lean not unto your own understanding. Remember that God, Christ, and the Holy Spirit work together to help us run our race. Christ gave us the model. God gives us the test, and the Holy Spirit teaches us what to do. Your book recommendation for this chapter is *The Apostle: A Life of Paul*. Paul gives us a shining example of what it looks like to go through trials and how to use those trials to make ourselves stronger and continue running our race. His life is amazing and deserves to be studied by every Christian.

We must trust the perfection of the creation so far, as to believe that whatever curiosity the order of things has awakened in our minds, the order of things can satisfy.[1]

—Ralph Waldo Emerson

Don't worry about anything; instead, pray about everything. Tell God what you need, and thank him for all he has done.

—Philippians 4:6

Chapter 7

In order to accomplish all the goals we have set for ourselves, the main one being excellence achieved by creating virtuous habits, which will in turn lead to our overall joy, we need to understand a few things about God and the order of the world. One thing we must gleam in order to be successful in our pursuit of joy is the importance of trust. We must understand that God can be and must be trusted in order to achieve joy. If you do not trust God, you cannot have joy, for you will spend countless hours in anxiety and worry. Truly there is so much to worry about. We could die at any moment of every day from the hands of other humans, natural disaster, or sickness in our bodies. Once we get past the worry of death, we may feel anxiety over the afterlife. Is there really a heaven? Will my sin on earth keep me out of heaven? Innumerable questions and concerns can and do plague us without trust in God.

God has positioned us to be totally dependent. All true power lies in God's hands, and we are only given free will to choose our actions, not our situations. But in our powerlessness, we can be free. We can be free with the knowledge that there is a creator who is caring for us and who is deeply concerned about every minute aspect of our lives. When we stop worrying and start trusting, we can be free from anxiety. God has created us to be infants, completely dependent but also completely carefree. We need never worry, for at all times we are cared for, and even when it looks as if our situation is bleak, we can stand on the promises of God and know that this too is for our good. In his book *Your Best Life*

Now, Joel Osteen talks about trusting God rather than worrying. Osteen says that God will sometimes purposefully put us into situations that make us uncomfortable because there is something we are meant to do while we are there. We often complain when we find ourselves in these situations until we realize that we are in the perfect place to be used by God and help someone else. Osteen reminds us that no matter what the situation, God is in control and has our best interest at heart. Just like infants, we can live free from worry or care. We are told time and time again in the Bible to lay our burdens before the Lord, who knows what we have need of and who will fight all our battles. This is repeated so often because it is an important concept. God wants nothing more than to be trusted and relied on completely, even and especially in our toughest of times.[2]

Trust is the key to our overall joy. When man was originally created, God had him living in a perfect paradise with no need to work or to worry. When sin came into the world, worry and anxiety came with it. In fact, worry itself is a sin because it says that you do not trust the Creator of the universe to handle the situation. Leon Shenandoah, a Tadodaho Indian chief, tells us that worrying only upsets God, and it actually keeps things from happening as quickly as they could if we would simply trust God to do what he said he would do. As we have mentioned before, all sin separates you from God, who is without sin, and that is exactly the problem with worry. It separates you from God. How can you be connected to God if you doubt the Almighty's ability to handle the situation? Now I am not saying it is easy to just let go of all worry and concern. I know it is not. I am not saying it's easy. *I am saying it is worth it.* Giving God the burden of figuring out how things are going to work out makes your life incredibly calmer. If you could simply say, "God's got it," every time a trial came into your life, you would have no worries, and you would achieve joy and peace. After all, we know from experience that

God does have it and always will. So why is it that we continue to worry? Why can't we let go?[3]

We worry because we want to be in control. We have convinced ourselves that our actions lead to certain reactions in the world. If we work hard, if we are good, if we save our money, then we won't have trials or financial hardship. Of course, this is all a lie. Now don't get me wrong. I do believe in working diligently and achieving moral excellence and fiscal responsibility, but I have the good sense to know that these things will not save me. They will not save me from disaster here on earth, and they will not save me in the hereafter. I can work hard, be good, and make good financial decisions only to have a tornado rip through my home or bandits rob me of my possessions, or the company I work for could shut down and lay me off. I cannot control the world. And no matter how well I behave toward my fellow man, if I have no relationship with Christ, I cannot guarantee a place for my soul in heaven. I have no control over the world. My only control is over my own soul. I can control my thoughts, my heart, and my spirit. And when I turn these things toward God and focus on the things I can control, I no longer have to worry. Obedience to God is all I need to concern myself with. Christ tells us to "seek ye first the kingdom of God and his righteousness; and all these things shall be added unto you" (Matthew 6:33 KJV). This means that if we focus on God, all our needs will be provided. Now again I know it is easier said than done. Just like it is with our other virtues, trust in God will take practice. Lucky for us God wants us to succeed. Thus, we have lots of opportunities for practice. The trick is to see them that way, not as burdens or trials but opportunities to trust God.

Here's some practical advice about what to do when you catch yourself worrying, and it's much the same as it would be in the times when you catch yourself focusing on small sin. Acknowledge that you were worrying and that you were wrong for doing it. Ask God to forgive you and to take the doubt out of you. And finally shift your thoughts and fill yourself with words of trust. I suggest reading Scriptures that speak on the topic of worry. The following Scriptures are recommended: Psalm 55:22–23, Matthew 6:27–34, John 14:1–4, and Philippians 4:19–20. Mark these in your Bible and refer to them when you catch yourself worrying. Let the Word of God be your strength.

Two more quotes from Christ are especially useful to me. When I am worrying about bills or obtaining a job, really anything to do with finances, I read this quote from Luke 12:22–24:

> Then, turning to his disciples, Jesus said, "That is why I tell you not to worry about everyday life— whether you have enough food to eat or enough clothes to wear. For life is more than food, and your body more than clothing. Look at the ravens. They don't plant or harvest or store food in barns, for God feeds them. And you are far more valuable to him than any birds!"

When we put our financial hardship in perspective and think about how God cares for all creatures, we begin to see how foolish our worry is. God created everything and is more than capable of providing for all of earth's creatures.

Another great quote from Christ can be found in Matthew 10:28–31. I use this quote when I am anxious and afraid for my life. If someone or something is threatening me, I read the following

> Don't be afraid of those who want to kill your body; they cannot touch your soul. Fear only God, who can destroy both soul and body in hell. What is the price of two sparrows—one copper coin? But not a single sparrow can fall to the ground without your Father knowing it. And the very

hairs on your head are all numbered. So don't be
afraid; you are more valuable to God than a whole
flock of sparrows.

I find this quote to be a great comfort when there is a bad
storm or extreme weather warning. We must remember that
God is omnipresent and all-powerful. No mishap can befall us
without God having knowledge of it, and if God knows about
it and allows it, then it must be for our good. I love that both of
the previous quotes involve comparing your life to that of a bird.
When we use comparison to view the difficulties in our lives, we
quickly see how things could most certainly be worse, and we
thank God for the blessings we have. I recommend memorizing
both of the previous verses to encourage yourself when you find
that you are becoming anxious or worried.

Remember that it is the enemy's job to kill, steal, and destroy
our joy. We cannot allow this to happen. We must force ourselves
to recognize those moments when fear and worry begin creeping
upon us, and we must know that these emotions are not of God.
The enemy knows that we are sinning and separated from God
when we worry. In order to fight the enemy's attacks, we must be
vigilant, knowledgeable, and filled with the Word of God, which
is our weapon against the enemy. Hebrews 10:35–39 says,

> So do not throw away this confident trust in the
> Lord. Remember the great reward it brings you!
> Patient endurance is what you need now, so that
> you will continue to do God's will. Then you will
> receive all that he has promised. "For in just a
> little while, the Coming One will come and not
> delay. And my righteous ones will live by faith.
> But I will take no pleasure in anyone who turns
> away." But we are not like those who turn away

from God to their own destruction. We are the faithful ones, whose souls will be saved.

You have to remember your reward. You have to trust God if you wish to have joy. It is important, and it is worth your time to get into the habit of trusting God. Again, remember that complete trust in God won't happen overnight. You must work at it. The better you get at it, the larger the challenges you will face, and the more the enemy will fight you, but when you embrace trust instead of worry, you will be carefree and live the way God intended for you to live. This chapter's book recommendation is *Your Best Life Now* by Joel Osteen. I exhort you to focus on the chapters pertaining to trust and apply them to your life.

He answered one of them, "Friend, I haven't been unfair! Didn't you agree to work all day for the usual wage? Take your money and go. I wanted to pay this last worker the same as you. Is it against the law for me to do what I want with my money? Should you be jealous because I am kind to others?" So those who are last now will be first then, and those who are first will be last.

—Matthew 10:13–16

Chapter 8

A large part of trusting God is accepting the circumstances and situations we are born into. Not everyone's childhood was ideal. Many of us suffered in childhood through no fault of our own. We were victims at the hands of the people who should have been protecting us. Those conditions shaped us and created the adults we became. In order to trust God, we must not only rely on God in our daily lives but also accept those things that have happened in our past and over which we have no control. We must learn to accept mistreatment from others as a part of our Christian race.

I chose to focus on childhood first because it is the time in our lives when we have the least amount of power and control over our circumstances. It often seems that the injustices done to us in childhood hurt much more than those we suffer as adults. However, no matter at which age we suffer injustice, our reaction should be the same. We must continue to trust God and accept that what is happening or has happened to us is for our good. This can be very hard to do, as it is easy to lash out and harbor hate in your heart for a *person* who has done you wrong. If it were merely unfortunate circumstances causing our suffering, it would be simpler to move on, but when individuals hurt us, they give us people to hate. When people abuse us, steal from us, or hurt us emotionally, it can be difficult to overcome and forgive. In these times trust in God has to be the second step.

The first step will always be acceptance—both acceptance that the incident has actually happened and acceptance that God will work the situation out for our good. The first part can be the most difficult. It may not seem that way at first glance, but think about the most horrible thing that has happened to you. I can almost guarantee that it happened to you at the hands of someone else, and even now you have a hard time bringing it to mind because you spend so much time pushing it down and trying to forget. Even though you may have been devastated by the death of a loved one, the loss of a job, or the destruction of all your worldly goods, these public sufferings are not the most horrible thing for many people. These things happened, and they cannot be denied. They are horrible, but you did not suffer them alone. Others were aware of your circumstances and may have attempted comfort. But those personal attacks you received from another person were not public, and there was no one there to commiserate and provide comfort.

No one ever has to know about the sexual, physical, or emotional abuse you suffered behind closed doors. In fact, the easiest thing for you to do is pretend it never happened. It might still haunt you, but no one has to know. Do you see now what I mean by accepting it? Not all of us have had traumatic life experiences, and some of us who have had them have the good sense to talk to someone about them and try to heal. But unfortunately a great many more simply push these events down and do not heal from the pain. Until you deal with the injustice and allow God to heal the pain, you will not be able to achieve true joy because you will not be able to trust God. Until you come to terms with this pain, part of you will always be unable to forgive God for allowing the injustice in the first place. So we see that in order to trust God, we must accept our mistreatment.

Not only must we accept our mistreatment and know there is nothing we can do to reverse it, but in order to have true joy, we must come to the place where we become grateful to our enemy for the opportunity he or she provides for us to practice patience. His Holiness, the Dalai Lama tells us that without the opportunity provided to us by our enemies, we would not be able to perfect our virtue of patience. Truly we should be grateful to our enemy for providing us with the opportunity to practice. We must come to a place in our Christian race where we appreciate the injustices heaped upon us because they give us an opportunity to grow both closer to God and more like Christ spiritually. I know for many of you this seems like a real stretch, possibly the most difficult thing I have asked of you yet, but this is a critical part of our pursuit of perfection and moral excellence. It is easy to be perfect when everything in your life is perfect and no one is causing you harm of any kind, but that kind of perfection comes with no sacrifice. The people we as humans admire are the ones who suffered injustice and still choose to do the right thing. Those people who refuse to pay back evil with more evil but who conquer evil by doing good are the ones we esteem. Again, we look to our model, Jesus Christ, and all the injustices he suffered at the hands of men. He could have stopped it all with a word, but he chose to endure it. Not only did he persevere through his injustice, but he accepted it as a necessary part of his destiny and forgave his persecutors.[1]

We know that on the cross in his last dying words, Jesus asked that his oppressors be forgiven. His reason for forgiving them was that they knew not what they were doing. The same thing can be said for our persecutors. They too know not what they do when they commit injustice against us. If they could really imagine and feel the pain they were putting you through instead of focusing only on themselves and their pain, they would cease to hurt you. If they could see the situation from your perspective, they would not afflict you so. The point of this chapter can be boiled down to this quote from Paul in 1 Corinthians 6:7: "Even to have such lawsuits with one another is a defeat for you. Why not just accept the injustice and leave it at that? Why not let yourselves be cheated?" Part of trusting God is accepting mistreatment from other humans. It is going to happen. Christ told us that we would be hated for his sake. The sooner you accept this as a part of your race, the sooner you will be able to turn it into a blessing and use it for your good.

However, acceptance does not stop at the injustices committed by others. It also applies to the trespasses we ourselves have committed. For many of us, it is not what has been done to us but what we have done to others that haunt us. We cannot forgive ourselves, and we cannot believe God when we are told we are forgiven. Just as we must accept the actions of others, we must also accept our own past actions. This is often more difficult to do than forgiving someone else, as we tend to be our own worst judges. The process of accepting our own past actions and trusting God when we are told we are forgiven is the same as that for forgiving others. We must accept what we did and the fact that there is nothing that we can now do to take it away. We must talk to God about it and ask the Lord for forgiveness and peace. The Lord can give you peace over your own poor actions; however, you must accept what you have done, and you must trust God to forgive you.

In conclusion, in order to trust God, you must accept the mistreatment of others as a part of your race, and you must change your perspective on persecution so that you do not see it as a burden but as an opportunity. If you can do these things, you will be one step closer to fully trusting God and being free from all worry. This chapter's book recommendation is *The Art of Happiness* by the current and fourteenth Dalai Lama. I suggest you focus on the chapters about compassion and apply them to your life.

Brothers and sisters, we urge you to warn those who are lazy. Encourage those who are timid. Take tender care of those who are weak. Be patient with everyone. See that no one pays back evil for evil, but always try to do good to each other and to all people. Always be joyful. Never stop praying. Be thankful in all circumstances, for this is God's will for you who belong to Christ Jesus.

—1 Thessalonians 5:16–18

Chapter 9

Now we have accepted the fact that injustices will be heaped upon us as followers of Christ; however, we are still expected to trust God through these, and we should look at these injustices as blessings, as they provide us with the opportunity to practice patience and be more Christlike. With that in mind, we may be a little bit annoyed at God for expecting so much from us. This is understandable, though of course it is not justified. It is like your pets being mad at you for being away all day at work. They don't understand why you can't be with them all the time. All they want to do is give you love and affection, and yet you abandon them day in and out. You, on the other hand, understand that you have to go to work. If you did not go to work, there would be no home and no food. The suffering of your pet is necessary. But no matter what you do, you can never make your dog or cat understand this fact.

It is the same with us and God. God is so far above us in intelligence, wisdom, love, and who knows what else that we will never understand the true purpose of our suffering during our time on earth. What we do know, however, is that God is caring for us and that we should *be thankful* no matter what we are suffering. If we are going to be thankful, we must learn to look at not just what is happening or how we are feeling in the moment but at our entire lives and how God has been faithful to us in every aspect. The fact is that in every moment you have been provided for. There were times in your past when people hurt you and things looked bad, but through the grace and mercy of God, you came out of it. If God cared for you before, God will continue to care for you, and you have every reason to be thankful right now. God has proven to be faithful.

It amazes and appalls me how we can learn certain behavior and have faith in worldly things but not in God. We learn that when the light turns green at the intersection, we go, and when it turns red, we stop. We trust these rules, and every time we pull out into the intersection, we have faith that everyone will follow these rules—so much faith that half the time we are barely paying attention to our driving. We have this faith even though we know that car accidents kill an average of one hundred people every day. We have this faith in one another's adherence to the rules of the road, but we do not trust God to care for us. This is why we must have thankful hearts. When we learn to appreciate all of what God does for us, we will begin to see the little things that other people tend to miss. When we acknowledge God in these little things, we will develop the trust that is critical for our overall joy. Remember: in order to be free, we must be as infants, totally dependent on God. The fact is we already are totally dependent on God. God is the reason the earth's ecosystem works to give us life. No God, no oxygen. No oxygen, no life. God is the Creator and the Sustainer of *everything*. As Christians, we must admit our dependence on God and learn to be grateful for all that God does for us.

One of the best examples I can think of for learning to trust and appreciate God comes from *A Narrative of the Captivity and Restoration of Mrs. Mary Rowlandson*. This true account tells of the capture, imprisonment, and eventual release of Mrs. Mary Rowlandson. Mary was the wife of a minister living in Lancaster in the seventeenth century. On February 20, 1676, the Wampanoag Indians attacked Lancaster. Mary was captured and taken hostage for eleven weeks until she was eventually ransomed. Her narrative, which she wrote after her release, gives an account of her terrible ordeal. In her final paragraph, Mary shares some words of encouragement that are relevant to us today. Mary says,

The Lord hath showed me the vanity of these outward things. That they are the vanity of vanities, and vexation of spirit, that they are but a shadow, a blast, a bubble, and things of no continuance. That we must rely on God Himself, and our whole dependence must be upon Him. If trouble from smaller matters begin to arise in me, I have something at hand to check myself with, and say, why am I troubled? It was but the other day that if I had had the world, I would have given it for my freedom, or to have been a servant to a Christian. I have learned to look beyond present and smaller troubles, and to be quieted under them.[1]

The ordeal that Mary faced did not turn her away from God but instead taught her to trust and be thankful. Her whole perspective changed, and she was able to see that we must rely on God in all things. I love the words she uses, "Our whole dependence must be upon him." Again, she highlights our infant-like dependence on God. Many people would have been bitter and ungrateful if they had suffered as she had, but Mary had the good sense to be thankful to God for the experience, for it allowed her to see what was really important in life and to look past the petty smaller troubles. Mary was thankful and able to say that she had grown and improved because of her hardship. Though our personal hardships may not be a as great as Mary's, we must learn to look at how we have grown and improved from our own personal experiences of hardship in the same way she did, and as she did, when we recognize those moments, we must be thankful for them. We must look at these hardships and be grateful to God, who is molding us and making us more godlike.

But it is not only these big moments we must be thankful for. We must also be thankful for the small everyday things as well. Some things happen to us, and it is clear that only God could have saved us from those. But what about the little stuff? What about the everyday miracles that bless us and keep our lives running smoothly? If we are going to have thankful hearts, we must learn to recognize and appreciate these commonplace miracles as well. Every act of kindness committed toward us must be seen for what it is, an act of God. I love the way C. S. Lewis explains this concept. He compares acts of kindness from others to a baby taking its mother's milk. The baby just drinks without recognizing that the mother is doing this great thing for him or her, and so we too are not expected to recognize the hand of God behind acts of kindness originally. But eventually in our Christian walk, we must come to the place where we realize that it is not our neighbor who is doing this kind thing for us but rather God. If we believe simply in the kindness of man, we will undoubtedly be let down, as men are flawed individuals. Though we must be as infants in our trust and dependence on God, we must not be ignorant of God's place in our lives. Babies do not understand their relationship to their mothers. They simply take. It is only after growing older that the baby learns to be thankful. We cannot stay babies when it comes to the things of God. We must trust God, yes, but this does not mean we must be ignorant. Instead, we must be thankful in our knowledge, and in order to be thankful, we must recognize that God gives all good things.[2]

If we are going to acknowledge and give God praise for all the circumstances of our lives, both good and bad, we must begin by acknowledging the good. We must put in the effort of remembering and reflecting on the good in our lives. I suggest doing this during your daily prayer time. Yes, you should acknowledge your burdens and place them into God's hands, but after you empty yourself of burden, you need to fill yourself back up with the knowledge of God's goodness and a thankful heart. The more you do this, the easier it will become to trust God no matter what the circumstances. This chapter's book recommendation is *A Narrative of the Captivity and Restoration of Mrs. Mary Rowlandson.* Mary's testimony is powerful, and it is a story that every Christian can learn from. It is a short but commanding tale that shows us that we must thank God even in the midst of the storm, and I pray that it inspires and encourages you.

And I saw the sacred hoop of my people was one of
many hoops that made one circle, wide as daylight
and as starlight, and in the center grew one mighty
flowering tree to shelter all the children of one mother
and one father. And I saw that it was holy.[1]

—Black Elk Speaks

Chapter 10

Now I would like to begin giving you some practical advice. Up until now we have spoken in a very abstract way. We have compared life to a race with its ups and downs, and we have discussed the nature of joy and the constancy of suffering. But most of what we have discussed has involved concepts to meditate on but not mandates to follow. Personally I believe you must learn and understand these abstract concepts before you can begin successfully living them out. Consequently I am glad we have covered them, and I hope you have had time to ponder them. Now that we are moving into the practical realm, the first subject I want to approach is believing that you are a part of God's family.

When you become a follower of Christ, you are immediately adopted into the family of God. We know this because Paul says so in Romans 8:15–17. He states that "you have not received a spirit that makes you fearful slaves. Instead, you received God's Spirit when he adopted you as his own children. Now we call him, 'Abba, Father.' For his Spirit joins with our spirit to affirm that we are God's children. And since we are his children, we are his heirs. In fact, together with Christ we are heirs of God's glory. But if we are to share his glory, we must also share his suffering." Through a relationship with Christ, you convert from being God's creation to God's child. This is a step that I think many Christians miss, which is unfortunate because making this shift changes the way one behaves toward God. When you were in the world and had an idea of God but not a relationship, you thought of God as

Creator, judge, bringer of good things, and possibly some other less appealing titles. You based your relationship on these titles. God the Creator really only affects you when you are out in nature, enjoying the general splendor. God, who always gives good things, can be thanked in those moments we receive mercy and grace, like when we don't get the speeding ticket we deserve or when the car flips three times on the interstate but somehow you make it out alive. Finally there is God the judge who is watching us. He sees our sin and convicts us for our wrong actions. These are all attributes of God, and they are universal to all who believe; however, the truth is God is so much more.

In order for us to live out these principles that will lead to our joy, we must shift the way we see God and one another. We must see God as Father and others as siblings. Once we are able to change our perspective this way, it will also change our behavior. In order to help us make this shift in perspective, we need to look at what it means to be a father. For many of us this is not as easy as it sounds. A great number of us grew up fatherless and do not have a good example of what a father looks like. So for those of us who fall into that category, let us discuss it. First of all a father creates. The father is the creator of the child, and our heavenly Father is the Creator of all known things. That part you already knew, I am sure. Secondly a father protects. Fathers literally keep danger away from children—danger from outside forces or danger that children get themselves into out of ignorance. Our heavenly Father also protects us from danger. Sometimes the danger is seen, and sometimes it is not seen.

Next a father provides. He provides shelter, food, warmth, and much more. Our heavenly Father is also a provider, and he provides all the elements needed to keep our bodies alive, including but not limited to oxygen, sunlight, rain, and plant life. After these physical comforts and needs, our fathers also provide love. This is a big step. A lot of us don't get it from our earthly fathers, and some of us don't believe we get it from our heavenly

Father. Love is crucial for a person to grow up healthy and whole. Children who never experience the love of fathers will grow up with something missing, and this missing element will affect them as adults. We often call the effects of this missing element "daddy issues." This is true for males and females. Fortunately for us, though our earthly fathers may let us down in the arena of love, our heavenly Father never will.

This view of God as Father is an awesome revelation, but for many it is hard to imagine. It is hard to imagine because we put God on a pedestal, but we do not allow God to be our Father. For example, we expect certain things from our fathers here on earth. We should be able to say, "Daddy, help me! Dad, I need this. Why, Dad?" and receive an immediate answer. We demand all these things of our earthly fathers but clam up when it comes to God, our heavenly Father. We do this because we imagine that God is too busy or just plain to far above our small daily issues. This, however, is wrong and not what God wants from us. Paul tells us in Galatians 3:24–29,

> The law was our guardian until Christ came; it protected us until we could be made right with God through faith. And now that the way of faith has come, we no longer need the law as our guardian. For you are all children of God through faith in Christ Jesus. And all who have been united with Christ in baptism have put on Christ, like putting on new clothes. There is no longer Jew or Gentile, slave or free, male and female. For you are all one in Christ Jesus. And now that you belong to Christ, you are the true children of Abraham. You are his heirs, and God's promise to Abraham belongs to you.

We have been enveloped by Christ, he says, and when God looks at us, it is through the lens of Christ, the Son. So we see then that there is no difference between our relationship with our heavenly Father and that of our earthly fathers, for we are as Christ, who is God's only begotten Son. The only difference is in the fact that our heavenly Father is perfect. So how much more should we look to our heavenly Father than our earthly fathers who are imperfect?

We should approach God not just for the big things and not just when we have problems, though of course we should in those times as well because God loves us as a father and wants to protect us. But we should also approach him when we are happy and want to share our good news with our Father or when we simply want to talk to someone. Because our Father loves us, our Father wants to be our confidant. That is why Christ brings us not into religion but into relationship with God. Because of Jesus, we can—and we are encouraged to—go to God with any and every issue, and we know that God is delighted to be of service to us. We are not bothering God when we do this as some people believe. God did not create us to then turn around and ignore us. God loves us and wants to be our Father. It is only our perspective that is holding us back from a loving relationship that would free us from worry and anxiety.

The final trait of a father is being a disciplinarian. Our fathers do a great deal to nurture and care for us when we are children, but because we are children, we are ignorant of the way we should behave in the world. Our fathers on earth know what the right ways, are and they endeavor to teach us the correct way to behave. Sometimes in order to teach, they must use discipline. This discipline does not come out of anger or hate but love. Our fathers discipline us to protect us and to guide us into becoming healthy human beings. If a baby boy tries to put something into a socket and you tell him no, you do it because you do not want him to be hurt. You know that it could kill him. If he persist then you punish him in order to discourage him from destructive behavior. Now people might say, "Why don't you just get one of those socket covers?" And though that is a good idea, what are you going to do when the boy visits another family's home and they don't have socket covers? Danger is everywhere, and a child must not just be shielded from it but also taught to avoid it.

God is also a disciplinarian. Just like our fathers here on earth, God wants to help us avoid destructive behavior. Many times when there are trials and tribulations in our adult lives, these are the result of being disciplined by God. The problem for us as humans is that we do not see it that way. Unlike with an earthly father, there is no one standing over us, giving us a lecture on what we did wrong and why we deserve the beating. The conviction for our mistakes comes through the Word of God, the Holy Spirit, and sometimes an outside source like a pastor, but it is not nearly as obvious a thing as being punished by one's earthly father. This is why having time set aside every day for prayer and communing with God is critical. During this time we should reflect on our previous day. If there was a trial or test in that day, we must reflect on it and try to discern why God allowed it. What was its purpose? What can be gained by it? These are the questions to ask of yourself and of God. You might think this is overkill, but I guarantee you it is not. Remember to take God off of the pedestal! God cares about the intimate details of your life, not just the big things, and everything with God happens for a reason. We know this is true of God because Hebrews 12:6–9 says,

> For the Lord disciplines those he loves, and he punishes each one he accepts as his child. As you endure this divine discipline, remember that God is treating you as his own children. Who ever heard of a child who is never disciplined by its father? If God doesn't discipline you as he does all of his children, it means that you are illegitimate

and are not really his children at all. Since we respected our earthly fathers who disciplined us, shouldn't we submit even more to the discipline of the Father of our spirits, and live forever?

From this quote we can see that God's training is really just an extension of God's love for us. With God, there is no question about love. The Bible tells us that God gave his only begotten Son out of love for us. As believers in Christ, we become children of God, so now God loves us not as the creation but as begotten children. So of course as the children of God, we have to be trained to stop our destructive sticking-things-in-the-light-socket behavior and instead become mature Christian adults who seek perfection and reflect God back to God.

Oftentimes our fathers on earth are training their children not to be just like themselves but to be better than themselves. They recognize that they have made costly mistakes, and they wish to prevent the children they love from making the same mistakes. With God, however, there is no error, so when God trains you, he does so toward perfection. Thus, you should be grateful that God thinks so highly of you as to believe *you can be perfect*.

Now that we are coming to the end of this chapter, let us summarize what it is we are going to do in the future because we have learned that God is our Father. First we are going to believe in our hearts that we are the children of God, and as such, we are going to treat God differently. We are going to take God off of the pedestal and develop a true father-child relationship by meditating on the Scriptures Galatians 3:24–28, Romans 8:15–17, and Hebrews 12:1–9. Secondly we will treat God, our Father, as a confidant whom we can speak with at any time about any issue in perfect truth. We are not going to lie or sugarcoat the situation when we talk to God because we know our Father loves us and simply desires to help us. We will talk to our Father in this manner during the time we have set aside each day for prayer, meditation, and reflection. Finally we will submit to God's training just as we would our earthly father's, keeping in mind the knowledge that all discipline comes from a place of love. This chapter's book recommendation is *Christian Behavior* by C. S. Lewis. I want to highlight chapters 9 through 12 especially. I exhort you to focus on the areas that speak about God's love, and as always, I hope you are blessed.

Look here, you who say, "Today or tomorrow we are going to a certain town and will stay there a year. We will do business there and make a profit." How do you know what your life will be like tomorrow? Your life is like the morning fog—it's here a little while, then it's gone. What you ought to say is, "If the Lord wants us to, we will live and do this or that." Otherwise you are boasting about your own pretentious plans, and all such boasting is evil.

—James 4:13–16

Chapter 11

Yet another shift we must make in order to free our minds from the shackles of this world is apparent in the way we approach life. We have spoken about viewing our lives as races and ourselves as runners with a goal in mind, but that can be difficult to do at times. The enemy knows that a goal-oriented Christian is bad for business, so the enemy concocts schemes and devices to distract you from your goals and purpose. The enemy is very good at his job. He was doing it for thousands of years before you were even born. Thus, defeating him at this game is going to take a lot of effort on your part. You will have to be intentional in the way you live your life and in the way you allow yourself to think, for our thoughts influence our actions.

In order to be successful in overcoming the enemy's siege against your purpose and destiny, you must develop a sense of your own mortality. You must live always with the knowledge that today may be your very last day on earth. It cannot just be present in the back of your mind, but it must be on the cusp, influencing your actions. Now I am sure you think that this is a pretty morbid way to live, but it is not really so morbid to a Christian who believes in a life eternal with one's heavenly father. If you truly believe in the promises of God, you should not fear death, which is simply a transition from one place to another. However, I understand that this may be easier said than done, and I will remind you that we are learning new habits here and that nothing happens overnight. You must build this virtue just like you would any other by behaving *as if* you do not fear it, even though you do. If you behave as if you are not afraid long enough, eventually you will not be afraid.

Now to begin your next argument, you may ask, "Where do I find this in the Bible? I do not remember the passage that says that we must dwell at all times on our impending death." Of course you are correct about this, as there is no passage that I am aware of that openly says this. However, I believe it is plainly stated in several places, including Matthew 24. As Christ gives many parables to describe the suddenness of the coming of the Son of Man, he repeatedly exhorts the disciples to be ready and to look for signs of the end times. My favorite part of these parables concerns the watchful house owner. "So you, too, must keep watch! For you don't know what day your Lord is coming. Understand this: If a homeowner knew exactly when a burglar was coming, he would keep watch and not permit his house to be broken into. You also must be ready all the time, for the Son of Man will come when least expected" (Matthew 24:42–44). I like this parable because it is simple and easy for anyone to understand. Basically it is saying you must always be ready because you do not know when the end is coming. If you knew it was coming today, you would prepare, but since you do not know, you must always be prepared. *You must live your life prepared.* We see now why prepared Christians walk around with the knowledge that any day may be the day of Christ's return and their last on earth.

Once you have made this mental shift, you will be better able to fight off distractions from the enemy because now you can focus on what is important. The knowledge that we are going to die soon keeps us from taking life for granted. We have to begin working toward virtue today, for we have a limited amount of time to get it right. As a Christian, you are striving toward a single and unique purpose in life. We must remember that our one true purpose in this life is to save our souls and to do God's holy will, for as Christ says in Matthew 16:26, "What do you benefit if you gain the whole world but lose your own soul? Is anything worth more than your soul?" The saving of your soul is your life's purpose, and the knowledge and state of being in God's holy will is what gives your life joy.

The distractions that come from the enemy and this world are simply tricks meant to sway you from the path of righteousness and purpose. If you knew that today was your last day, you would live without sin. You would love your brother and sister as yourself, and you would probably not go to work or do any chores. Because we do not know what day is our last, we cannot quit working. We must continue to work diligently as we are called to do by God. What we can do is fully embrace purpose and righteousness. With the knowledge of our mortality, we can run our race to the best of our abilities every day, and we can avoid distraction from the enemy.

So again I exhort you to carry your mortality around with you everywhere, not because of some morbid philosophical existentialism but because you want to live in every moment and you know that living requires staying in purpose and in communion with God. When worry arises from smaller troubles, dash them aside with the knowledge that this day may be your last. Remember that you need to give God your obedience, trust, and thanks no matter what the circumstances. As Job said, "The Lord gave, and the Lord hath taken away; blessed be the name of the Lord" (Job 1:21 KJV). The book recommendation for this chapter is *Making Good Habits, Breaking Bad Ones* by Joyce Meyer. As we transition into our next chapter, we will begin discussing the habits that will help bring us to joy. Reading Joyce Meyer's book will help you understand the importance of habits in your own life.

Don't use foul or abusive language. Let everything you say be good and helpful, so that your words will be an encouragement to those who hear them.

—Ephesians 4:29

Chapter 12

The next practical habit we are going to build has to do with words. A large part of being virtuous and godlike has to do with the words you say. Remember: Christ told us that it is not what goes into the body but what comes out of it that defiles it. The words we use with one another and those we speak over ourselves are very powerful. After all, God created the world through words. They are a powerful force for either good or evil, and they should always be used carefully. The book of James goes into great detail as to how important it is to control one's words as a Christian. James 1:26–27 tells us, "If you claim to be religious but don't control your tongue, you are fooling yourself, and your religion is worthless. Pure and genuine religion in the sight of God the Father means caring for orphans and widows in their distress and refusing to let the world corrupt you." This passage from James is saying quite a lot, so let us break it down.

First James states, "If you claim to be religious," so we must establish that this passage most definitely applies to us, as we claim to be followers of Christ. Next he tells us that if we do not control our sharp tongues, we are fooling ourselves, and our religion is not worth much. This seems rather harsh. Not only are we dropping the ball, but we are also lying to ourselves about it. As harsh as this may seem, is not James correct? When we fuss and cuss and say all manner of vile things, are we behaving Christlike? Is that kind of behavior leading people to Christ as we are commissioned to do in the final chapter of Matthew? No, it is not. If anything, it is giving those people who choose not to believe in Christ an excuse. They can excuse themselves by pointing at us and saying, "Look at how that so-called Christian behaves. How is he or she any different from me as a non-Christian? What is a relationship with Christ doing for them?" Thus, we see how our religion is not worth much when we don't control our tongues. It may not be hurting *us*, but it is not helping others come to Christ.

Next James declares that Christians who are pure and without fault do the following: They remain true to the Lord and are not soiled or dirtied by contact with the world. Again, we are reminded of the words of Christ and how what comes out of the body defiles it and makes it impure. Evil words have a direct correlation to the desolation of not only the spirit but also the body. In both the words of James and Jesus, we are told that the body loses its purity and deteriorates. Now you might think, *What do words have to do with our physical bodies?* The truth is that all flesh and blood was created by words, and these powerful words have the ability to give the body strength or to break it down. Just like when you are lifting weights or running laps, you will eventually feel fatigue. Soon you might think that it is time to rest, but if a friend or a trainer comes up and speaks words over you, pushing you to do just a little more, you will find that you have the strength to do it. The words themselves strengthen your body. Now that was a very practical analogy. The truth is that the power of words works in very impractical ways.

The effect of bad words on our bodies can be seen in many ways. It usually plays itself out in the symptoms of stress and anxiety. When people talk about us negatively, it can often change our self-images and lower our self-esteem and can lead to anxiety over every action we take. When we make playful but negative comments about one another, we are basically bullying each other. It might not seem that way at the time when someone makes a simple comment about your height or the way you walk. We often brush off little things like that, but over time they can become compounded and lead to stress and anxiety. You may think that everyone picks on other people a little and that it is all in good fun, but I submit that even though we all do it, that does not make it right. Step back a moment and consider our model, Jesus. Do you really think he would make comments about people's height, weight, or skin color, or would he be more concerned about their souls? Would Jesus criticize the way a person walks, or would he be too busy compelling them to walk with him? Our negative words do cause side effects not only to others but to ourselves as well and they are not representative of Christ.

James ends his passage by saying that true Christians remain loyal to the Lord and are not affected by contact with the world. Foul talk, we understand, is a result of contact with the world. It is not our natural propensity. We learn language from the people around us. If we spoke a heavenly language, I am convinced there would be no words of negativity in our vocabulary. Unfortunately the languages we currently speak include all manner of vile words and phrases, and these are the words we must remove from our vocabulary if we are going to be perfect as God hopes us to be. We cannot afford to use the world's foul language over ourselves. Nor can we speak it over the people who surround us. After all, the people around us are always more than they seem.

The Bible cautions us to be careful, for many have entertained angels unknowingly, but I say you should concern yourself not just with angels but with other people as well because people, including you, are more than what they seem. I like how C. S. Lewis phrases it. Lewis believes that people are holy. The people we interact with every day were created by God and are thus holy eternal beings and should be treated as such. I think we often forget that each of us is an immortal creation of God and that every single one of us is loved by God. In order to show God our love in return, we are asked to love others as ourselves. After all, they are also the immortal children of God who receive mercy and grace. Our neighbors deserve our mercy because God was merciful with us, and we must return the favor. Thus, we should not use bad language and should try to avoid anger with our neighbors. All our words over our neighbors should express life, not death.[1]

In conclusion, we will go forward and carefully choose our words so that we remain true to the Lord and not contaminated by the world. We will do this because we understand the power of words to shape destiny. We will be careful not only of the words we speak over ourselves but also of those we speak over others because the people around us are the holy creations of God. We show God our love by following Christ's commandment to love our neighbors as ourselves. We know that this transformation of our vocabulary will not happen overnight, but it is yet another virtuous habit we must build in order to be perfect and godlike, which is the only way to stay in constant communion with God and thus have joy. We will combat our negative thoughts, which lead to negative words, by filling ourselves with the Word of God, which is a mighty weapon against the enemy. The book recommendation for this chapter is the book of James in the Bible. This book gives great revelation on the power of the tongue, and it should be used as a shield against contact with the world and its negative vocabulary.

And don't sin by letting anger control you. Don't let the sun go down while you are still angry, for anger gives a foothold to the devil.

—Ephesians 5:26–27

Chapter 13

Related to our last topic involving words and how we use them wisely, anger and arguing are also relevant to our conversation about joy. One of the most obvious and important shifts we must make has to do with our views on these two issues. I talk about them in the same breath because they are more connected than we choose to believe. According to Merriam Webster *anger* is "a strong feeling of being upset or annoyed because of something wrong or bad." The word *argue* is a verb meaning "to disagree or fight by using angry words." Arguing is disagreement. It is a level past discussion, and it is a gateway drug that can lead to anger.

Now some of you may not have a problem with arguing, and thus, this chapter may not be of much use to you; however, all of us argue from time to time, and some of us have an arguing addiction. We all know that we are to avoid *anger*, which is wrong, and that God is in charge of wrath and vengeance, but I submit that we need to be wary of arguing as well. Philippians 2:14–15 says, "Do everything without complaining and arguing, so that no one can criticize you. Live clean, innocent lives as children of God, shining like bright lights in a world full of crooked and perverse people." We are called to shine out in a dark world, and the way we do that is by not complaining or arguing and not giving into the world's way of doing things. Of course, I am not saying that you simply give in and do not choose right over wrong. You must certainly stand up against the enemy, but you are to do this calmly and through the inarguable Word of God. Now there are those who will argue against the Word of God, but you cannot allow these deceived people to cause you to sin. Remember, "You must all be quick to listen, slow to speak, and slow to get angry. Human anger does not produce the righteousness God desires" (James 1:19–20). We cannot let the enemy trick us into arguing with him because our arguing can and often does lead to anger.

I am sure there are some of you who believe yourself capable of arguing without becoming angry, and perhaps you are; however, I believe it is unlikely, and furthermore, the Bible supports that opinion. Second Timothy 2:23–25 reads, "Again I say, don't get involved in foolish, ignorant arguments that only start fights. A servant of the Lord must not quarrel but must be kind to everyone, be able to teach, and be patient with difficult people. Gently instruct those who oppose the truth. Perhaps God will change those people's hearts, and they will learn the truth." Even though *you* are capable of avoiding anger while you are arguing, others may not be. Moreover, when you are arguing, you are most likely *not* being humble. It's more likely that you are asserting you know something the other person does not. This is opposed to God's will, for we are called to be patient teachers of those who are wrong just as the quote from Timothy says. When you argue, you are neither patient nor humble, and your actions are foolish, as you are not likely to persuade anyone who is angry. Again we are not talking about a simple discussion here. We all know that there is a point when discussion can be elevated to argument, and it is the point when anger enters the equation. That is why the two are so closely connected. The conversation was not an argument until one of the two parties became emotionally involved either because he or she felt belittled or because an emotional chord was hit in the conversation. Either way, we have now moved into the realm of argument, and very little progress can be made at this level.

If you find that an argument has snuck up on you either because *you* became emotional or the other person did, you must stop taking about the topic immediately. This can be very difficult, as we all enjoy being right, and walking away from an argument leaves it open for the other party to believe he or she is right. Even though you may believe you are right in your heart, you cannot let the Devil taunt you into staying in the argument. Sometimes we have to rise above a situation and let others believe they have bested us. Remember that our relationship with the Lord is the most important thing. Sometimes in order to stay in good standing with the Lord, we must allow others to feel that they have outdone us. Being able to this is a sign of a mature Christian. It is not easy, but it is good. God will bless you for doing so.

So again, once we realize the discussion has become an argument, we must discontinue the conversation, calmly tell the other party that you no longer wish to discuss the issue, and if it is necessary, you will revisit the conversation at a later date. If you are able, just walk away and find a quiet place to sit and talk to God. If you do not have the ability to walk away from the person, then you must redirect the energy. Offer him or her a choice. "We can either do this or that." Make it something that has nothing to do with what you were discussing. "We can either have pizza or Chinese for diner. What would you like?' Hopefully giving the other party the authority to make a choice will help him or her feel empowered and help the person to move past the argument. Of course, this will not always work, for the enemy does not want you to have joy. But no matter what, you must remember God's Word. If you are truly committed to being free from anger and arguing, you *will* accomplish your goal. The reading for this chapter is Matthew 5:21–26.

Don't love money; be satisfied with what you have. For God has said, "I will never fail you. I will never abandon you." So we can say with confidence, "The Lord is my helper, so I will have no fear. What can mere people do to me?"

—Hebrews 13:5–6

Chapter 14

Closely related to our last topic of anger and arguing is money. Money and the love of it are the cause of a large portion of sin in the world. Of course, like many other things, this is based on a mistaken belief system. It is the belief that if you have money, you are safe. The love of money comes from a desire for safety and is born out of fear. After a while the need for safety can vanish, and the fear can transition into a love of power and the influence that comes with money. For most of us, however, this will never be a problem. We will never have enough money to move past the realm of fear, but that does not mean that we do not love money. It is a universal truth that having money makes us feel secure. Unfortunately this is a false sense of security. Just think about any movie about natural disaster or zombie attacks. Is money any good to anyone then? Are people able to buy their ways out of the alien takeover? No, because money is senseless when our societal systems break down. If these examples are too abstract for you, think about Hurricane Katrina. Did money save anyone who was trapped in that situation? All the money they had became useless to them. If they wanted life's necessities, they had to take them. No currency was exchanged when people were fighting to survive. The sense of security that comes with having money is false. Then you may ask, "On what or in whom should we rely on to make us feel secure?" You guessed it—God Almighty.

God has promised to be our provider. There are numerous narratives in the Bible that exclaim how God saved people from death by starvation, lion, or flood, just to name a few. We must learn from these accounts and put our trust completely in God if we want to feel secure. No amount of money will save us if it is not in God's will. By remembering this and speaking words of trust in God over ourselves, we can overcome those moments when fear creeps in. When bills are due or food is scarce, we must remember the Psalm 23. In order to be affective in our pursuit of joy, I believe every Christian should memorize that passage. Passages like this one help us to overcome fear and doubt. Remember that the Word of God is your sword against the enemy. Use it regularly and wisely.

Treasure is also related to money. Treasure does not always come in the form of money, but even the treasure that is not made up of silver and gold can be a stumbling block in our pursuit of joy. Treasure is defined by dictionary.com as "anything or person greatly valued or highly prized." In its verb form, it can mean "to regard or treat as precious; cherish" (dictionary.com). The Bible tells us that having treasure here on earth is a mistake. Christ himself says, "Don't store up treasures here on earth, where moths eat them and rust destroys them, and where thieves break in and steal. Store your treasures in heaven, where moths and rust cannot destroy, and thieves do not break in and steal. Wherever your treasure is, there the desires of your heart will also be" (Matthew 6:19–21). Jesus is not talking about stores of gold and silver necessarily but what you value most highly, what is important to you.

Currently you are reading this text, so I assume a relationship with Christ is important to you, but is it your treasure? Is there something or someone you would choose before God if you had to make that choice? This can be a tough reality to face, as many of us have children we love a great deal. We should love them, but even our own children should not come before God. God told Abraham to sacrifice Isaac. God allowed the death of every one of Job's children, and God sacrificed Jesus Christ, his only begotten

Son, to save the world from its sins. So I say to you that *even your child* cannot be your greatest treasure. Of course, you can still treasure your child. I am certainly not saying that children are not treasure, but like all good gifts, they come from God. God gave you the child, and God has the right to take your child away. More important than anything else in this entire world is your relationship with God. Remember that our joy will only come as a side effect of being in constant communion with God and being godlike. God gave us the example of sacrificing a child when he offered up Christ Jesus, so we cannot expect exemption from this fate if God so chooses to stretch us in this way. We are not being asked to do anything God has not already done.

The conclusion that I hope you have reached from this chapter is that money should have no place in your life goals. When it comes as a gift from God, we should treat it like what it is, a benefit of being a disciple of Christ. Money is a benefit and not the paycheck of a relationship with Christ. Obtaining money should not be our goal in life or in our Christian walk. First Timothy 6:7–10 exclaims,

> After all, we brought nothing with us when we came into the world, and we can't take anything with us when we leave it. So if we have enough food and clothing, let us be content. But people who long to be rich fall into temptation and are trapped by many foolish and harmful desires that plunge them into ruin and destruction. For the love of money is the root of all kinds of evil. And some people, craving money, have wandered from the true faith and pierced themselves with many sorrows.

So let us stay away from the love of money by strengthening our faith. If we put our faith in the Word of God and not the imaginary security that money provides, we will be well on our way to joy. Let us also remember to be careful with what we treasure so that our hearts are always in the right place. Finally I exhort you to read Psalm 23, which is a great comfort to me personally, and to look for other passages in the Bible that speak on how God will provide all your needs. Once you find them, try your best to memorize them to use as weapons against the enemy. The book recommendation is *Financial Peace* by David Ramsey. With knowledge comes power. If you want to put your money to good use, read the work of this God-fearing financial author.

Dear children keep away from anything that might take God's place in your hearts. Amen.

—1 John 5:21

You adulterers! Don't you realize that friendship with the world makes you an enemy of God? I say it again: If you want to be a friend of the world, you make yourself an enemy of God.

—James 4:4

Chapter 15

Even more dangerous than the love of money is the great pull of the secular world. When we get past the love of money, which comes from the false sense of security it brings, we move on to the love of status. More than the money itself, we love what the money can acquire for us, namely worldly things. Worldly things are those items and actions in our world that are not of God. These things have been corrupted by the enemy. And unfortunately too often worldly things are the things we want most to have or to do. The lifestyles we see on TV and in movies are the ones we want to emulate and the people we want most to be like. These things appeal to our carnal nature, and the enemy encourages us in them. Therefore, they are the things we must guard the most securely against, as they are a slippery slope on the ride toward sin. This can be most difficult because we are surrounded by the world and its temptations.

Oftentimes we as humans have an innate desire to be *cool* and *hip* as we perceive others. We look at other people who we believe to be *cool*, and we decide that they are happy. However, this is wrong, and in order to combat this mentality, we must uncover the lie, namely that the pleasures of the world will make you happy. This is false, and if we are to be disciples of Christ and if we are to have joy, then we must resign ourselves from the world, pick up our crosses, and follow him. We are told by Christ in Luke 14:26–27, "If you want to be my disciple, you must hate everyone else by comparison—your father and mother, wife and children, brothers and sisters—yes, even your own life. Otherwise, you cannot be my disciple. And if you do not carry your own cross and follow me, you cannot be my disciple." Paul goes further than this in Romans 12:2 and tells us that we must be new people saying, "Don't copy the behavior and customs of this world, but let God transform you into a new person by changing the way you think. Then you will learn to know God's will for you, which is good and pleasing and perfect." Paul wants us to learn how to move and behave in this world from our own experiences. This is important because when we look to the world for satisfaction, we are trying to learn from other's experiences, but God has given us each what we need to obtain joy and peace.

We see people on our televisions, and they appear to be happy, so we assume that they are; however, we have no way of knowing if they are indeed happy, for people in movies and in music videos are performing. There is no way to know what goes on after the cameras go off, and what we tend to hear in the media is fraught with tragedy. This is why the Lord tells Jeremiah,

> If you speak good words rather than worthless ones, you will be my spokesman. You must influence them; do not let them influence you! They will fight against you like an attacking army, but I will make you as secure as a fortified wall of bronze. They will not conquer you, for I am with you to protect and rescue you. I, the Lord, have spoken! Yes, I will certainly keep you safe from these wicked men. I will rescue you from their cruel hands. (Jeremiah 15:19–21)

As followers of Christ, we must not allow ourselves to be influenced by the enemy and the world. We are the light of the world because we have the Holy Spirit inside of us. We know the truth. It is the worldly who are lost and need guidance. They put on a great front of appearing carefree when truly they are stumbling in the dark. It is our responsibility to show them the light by living a life of righteousness devoted to the Lord. Of course, the worldly will resist the light. They do not want to see the light. Just as a person who has been sitting in a dark room cringes when the lights come on, the world's initial reaction is to push back and hide themselves from the truth, for it is easier to believe that you are worthless and no good than to believe you are valued and have a divine destiny. But once people become accustomed to the light, they will appreciate it. They will realize that they can see where they could not before.

Too often, however, we are so influenced by the world ourselves that we cannot bring light to those who need it. The enemy has tricked us into desiring worldly things. Christ tells us that we should seek first the kingdom of God and that all the things we need will be given to us. It is essential to our race that we are not pulled in by the world. In 1 John 2:15–17, we are told,

> Do not love this world nor the things it offers you, for when you love the world, you do not have the love of the Father in you. For the world offers only a craving for physical pleasure, a craving for everything we see, and pride in our achievements and possessions. These are not from the Father, but are from this world. And this world is fading away, along with everything that people crave. But anyone who does what pleases God will live forever.

In order for us to have joy, we must stay in purpose and constant connection to God. We cannot do this when we are seeking after the hollow pleasures of the evil world. So what then do we do to avoid forbidden things? We must resign ourselves from the world. In fact, we must give up our citizenship in the world in order to gain citizenship in heaven. The world for us as

Christians is the enemy's territory. It is run by the enemy, and we become enemy combatants when we accept Christ as our Lord and Savior. As visitors to this world (and not its citizens), we know that when we are ready to go home, we cannot bring with us any foreign substances that we picked up in the world. Just as customs does not let you bring anything you want into America from foreign nations, you cannot bring worldly things into heaven. Therefore, we must give up the things of this world *now* because our time here is only temporary. In order to give these things up, we must train ourselves to hate the things of this world. It will not be easy, but it is our best course of action.

In order to separate ourselves from the worldly, we must learn to hate worldly things. The best way I can think of to grow to hate something is through constantly remembering the negative consequences of participating in it. For example, there was a time in my life when I loved taking shots. It offered a quick buzz with minimum effort. Then I started having hangovers, and as they got worse, I wanted to take shots less and less. The idea of taking a shot now turns my stomach. I hate shots! By remembering the adverse consequences, I was able to train myself to hate them. Now I do my best to avoid them. Thus, with the knowledge of an action's negative consequences, we can overcome our desire for worldly things. Any worldly action is going to have some negative consequences, even if the consequences are simply separating you from God. The point is that you can use the consequences to keep you from committing the act.

We can also use the positive results of resigning from the world to spur us on. Every time we feel the ambition to do something forbidden to us as citizens of God's kingdom, we can fight it by remembering who we are as royal children of God. Say to yourself, "I am above such worldly things. I am a citizen of God's kingdom." If you speak this over yourself enough, eventually you will believe it, and it will become a part of you. As we have already said, words are powerful. As with all things, it won't be immediate or perfect, but the more you fill your life with meaningful actions, the less time you will have for worldly things.

You may not know what worldly things you covet in your life because they have become such a regular part of your life and you no longer see them as wrong. If this is the case, you may need to pray that the Holy Spirit reveals them to you. If you want a better understanding of your citizenship and alien status in this world, I recommend the book *What Christians Believe* by C. S. Lewis, specifically the chapter titled "The Invasion." Finally, remember the cost of discipleship given to us by Christ and found in Luke 14:33. And remember that you will stumble and fall, but you are only defeated when you decide not to get back up and try again.

I don't really understand myself, for I want to do what is right, but I don't do it. Instead, I do what I hate. But if I know that what I am doing is wrong, this shows that I agree that the law is good. So I am not the one doing wrong; it is sin living in me that does it.

—Romans 7:15–17

Chapter 16

The problem with trying to avoid worldly things is that they are all around us, tempting us at every turn. Just as Paul says in this chapter's opening quote, we often find ourselves doing those things that we hate. Even after we have trained ourselves to hate something, we can still occasionally find ourselves indulging in it. We commit those evil acts that we know are wrong even though we do not want to. The problem is temptation. When one is on a diet, it is easier to not eat sweets. If there are no sweets in the house, there is no temptation. But when you get to work and find out it is someone's birthday and there is cake, then it is no longer easy, for now there is temptation.

In the previous chapter, I mentioned how I now hate to take shots, and though this is true, I still find myself taking shots occasionally. Now it might be years between opportunities, but eventually I will go to a party and forget that I hate shots. As I watch all my peers indulging, I will convince myself that I can just have one and that won't be so bad. "After all," I tell myself, "I don't want to be the *only one* not taking a shot." Well, as you may imagine, this never goes according to plan, and the next day I must suffer the consequences of my evil behavior. "Why did I do it?" I ask myself every time, and every time I swear I will not do it again. And I don't for a couple of years. But sooner or later I forget, and the cycle starts again.

What is the variable here that makes me do wrong over and over again? It is temptation. The fact is that I would not have taken those shots if I had been at home or at church that night.

I was only tempted to take them because I was at a party, and at the party the enemy's constant evil influence and my own sinful nature conspired to overpower me. I was tempted, and I fell. The problem was placing myself in the midst of temptation. I knew that going to a party like that would be difficult for me. I should have chosen to stay home, but if I really wanted to go or could not avoid going, I should have been honest with God and myself about my shortcomings and prayed for strength to overcome temptation before I went to the party. Temptation can and should be overcome with honest and diligent prayer. James 1:12–15 says,

> God blesses those who patiently endure testing and temptation. Afterward they will receive the crown of life that God has promised to those who love him. And remember: when you are being tempted, do not say, "God is tempting me." God is never tempted to do wrong, and he never tempts anyone else. Temptation comes from our own desires, which entice us and drag us away. These desires give birth to sinful actions. And when sin is allowed to grow, it gives birth to death.

Thus, we see from the Scripture that it is possible to overcome temptation. As a matter of fact, not only is it possible, but it is a necessary skill to develop as a follower of Christ. As a disciple of Christ, you must learn to overcome temptation. You do this by making your top priority obedience to God.

If you choose to go somewhere that will hold known temptations for you, you must strengthen and prepare yourself ahead of time. You have to desire to overcome all temptation before you ever come up against it. You have to want to be obedient. Now you might think, *Obviously we* want *to be obedient* before *we sin right. It is just hard sometimes.* But I ask that you examine yourself and your motives truly. Do you really want to be obedient when you commit that worldly act? I know I don't. When I decide to take those shots, I do it in defiance. Now naturally I justify it in my mind and tell myself all kinds of lies to make it okay for me to do what I should not do, but they are still lies. Between my lies and the enemy's lies—remember that the enemy is always out to get us and separate us from God—I have sufficient grounds to disobey God and commit my sinful act. Afterward when I am again suffering the consequences of my sinful actions, I repent of my act of disobedience.

The problem comes from the lack of desire for obedience. It is not that we desire to do wrong. It is that the enemy knows what weaknesses we have and what temptations to put before us so that we do not want to do right. My pastor is always telling us that the enemy will not tempt you with something you do not like. This takes me back to my shot example. In regards to my most recent disappointment, I was at a party where the shots we were taking were delicious. They were cherry-flavored and coffee-flavored, and there were also JELL-O shots. These are all tasty things that I enjoy. Had it been tequila or whiskey, the temptation would not have existed because I truly despise those two forms of alcohol. But alas, the temptation came in a sweet and delicious package. I let the temptation overcome my desire to be obedient, and I gave in and did what I did not want to do. Thus, I was taken back a step in my race toward joy.

If we are going to avoid falling prey to temptation over and over again, we must fill ourselves with the knowledge that joy comes only from a relationship with God and that the pleasure we get from giving in to temptation does not last and is not worth the pain that it causes. We must meditate on these things daily if we are to succeed. Again, my pastor says that God has to be a priority in our lives in order for us to be successful. Obedience to God is a necessity, and you will not be obedient if a relationship with God is not your life's priority over and above your own wishes and desires. You will not be able to obey God and thus receive true joy if you do not move yourself out of the way and make God your priority and the most important person in your life. We have repeated this theme many times in this book and in several different ways because it is probably the most difficult thing you will ever have to do consciously, but once you do it, once you make that shift from your own selfishness to God, you will be at peace. You will have joy, and you will be happy that you did it.

As with all our new habits, overcoming temptation is not easy. My advice to you is to avoid places where you will be tempted, but I know that this is not always possible. In order to openly overcome temptation, you must engage in regular honest prayer, admitting your faults and asking for strength. You must be honest with yourself about the pet sins you are committing and don't want to give up. These will be the hardest to overcome, but with commitment and perseverance, you will defeat these as well. You will fall sometimes, but you cannot stay down. You must get back up, dust yourself off, and keep pressing toward the mark. For this chapter I recommend the book of Romans, which was written by Paul. It is a treasure trove of encouragement and honest reflection, and I encourage you to read it again as you meditate on defeating your life's temptations. I pray that you use it to overcome and to press on.

For the world offers only a craving for physical pleasure, a craving for everything we see, and pride in our achievements and possessions. These are not from the Father, but are from this world.

—1 John 2:16

Chapter 17

The final caution I want to leave with you concerns pride. Even after you have broken the habits of speaking carelessly, storing up treasure here on earth, relying on money to give you a feeling of security, coveting worldly things, and giving into temptation, you are still in danger of pride. Pride, the quintessential sin of the Pharisees, is a snare that Christians can easily fall into. By living their lives to fit every letter of the law—or at least telling others that they had—the Pharisees developed an heir of superiority. They believed that their piety made them better than others. They did not indulge in the sins of the common man, and because of this, they were superior. When Christ came, he showed the world how wrong these so-called righteous and pious men were when it came to the things of God. He told them that their hearts were far from God, even though they honored God with their lips.

The hole into which we can stumble as Christians who are trying to be righteous followers of Christ is pride. The closer we grow to God and the better we feel about ourselves and our decisions, the easier it is to become conceited and to develop feelings of superiority. This is yet another trick of the enemy and one of the most dastardly in my opinion. Even after we have given up all worldly things, we can fall into the trap of pride. "What exactly is pride?" you may ask. C. S. Lewis tells us that pride is not the same as self-esteem. It is good and right to have self-esteem, but pride is comparing oneself to others and finding them lacking in comparison. Basically it's looking down on others because they are not as wonderful as you are. Thus, we are not prideful just because we like ourselves. Liking yourself calls for looking in and making judgments based on one's relation to God. We become proud when we look outward, compare ourselves to others, and find them deficient.[1]

When we start judging the actions of others as less righteous or worthy than our own, that's when the pride comes in. This is where the Pharisees tripped up. They no longer cared about doing right because it pleased God but rather because it gave them the chance to look down on those around them and to lord their status over them. The goal of our obedience to God is the joy and peace that we will receive and the pleasure of hearing God say, "Thy good and faithful servant, well done." When we stop delighting in the praise from God and the inner joy we receive and instead delight in ourselves, we have been consumed by pride. As long as you are looking down on others, you can't see God above you.

In order to counteract the effects of pride, we need to stay in a place of humility. How does one do that? It's achieved through two methods. First you must remember yourself. You can call to remembrance those sins and transgressions you committed not too long ago. You need not make excuses for why it is okay for you to make *mistakes* and not for others. Moreover, you should not make judgment calls on what sins are greater than others. The Bible tells us that all sins are the same in the eyes of God, and we know that all sin separates us from God, who is without sin. Thus, all sins are equal in that they are all committed against God, who desires that we be godlike and sinless. Asking you to remember yourself does not mean I want you to wallow in your past sins. Once you have repented for sin, God has forgiven you, and you should forgive yourself. I am not saying you should wallow. Rather I am saying you should reflect. Confucius tells us, "By three methods we may learn wisdom: first, by reflection, which is noblest; second, by imitation, which is easiest; and third by experience, which is the bitterest." Reflection is good for the soul and helps us avoid repeating past mistakes. For example, we reflect on black history in February; however, if we were to wallow in the history of black people in America, it would become an obsession, and we would have a hard time living in our present and having hope for our future. Thus, in our pursuit of humility, we reflect on our past sin to remind ourselves that we are no better than others.

The second method to counteract pride rests in thinking about the righteousness of God and how much you pale in comparison. Blaise Pascal says, "Knowing God without knowing our own wretchedness makes for pride. Knowing our own wretchedness without knowing God makes for despair. Knowing Jesus Christ strikes the balance because he shows us both God and our own wretchedness."[2] If we only knew of God's existence and the fact that we are created by God, we would be quite conceited, thinking ourselves special for being created by such an almighty being. But when we juxtapose our wretched and sinful nature to God's perfection and goodness, we see that we have no reason to be proud or to feel worthy. If Jesus Christ declared that he himself was not good but only God was (and is) good, then how can we think for a second that we ourselves are something to delight in?

So work hard to be righteous, but do not forget that your purpose is to please God and that you can take no credit for your own holiness. Use the two methods we just discussed to counter feelings of pride, and when it rises up, remember that your brothers and sisters deserve your love, your forgiveness, and your humility, for God has forgiven you. I recommend you read the book *Christian Behavior* by C. S. Lewis. I specifically recommend the chapter titled "The Great Sin." Read this for a more clarifying view on the nature of pride.

Don't be selfish; don't try to impress others. Be humble, thinking of others as better than yourselves. Don't look out only for your own interests, but take an interest in others, too.

—Philippians 2:3–4

Chapter 18

Now that we have emptied ourselves out, we need to fill ourselves back up. Whenever you get rid of a bad habit, you are obligated to replace it with a good habit. You have to replace it so that you do not go back to your old ways out of boredom and confusion. Thus, we ended our last chapter with a plan to be humble instead of prideful. Humility is one of the greatest character traits we can adopt. Christ calls us to humility many times in the gospels. In Matthew 23:11–12, Jesus says, "The greatest among you must be a servant. But those who exalt themselves will be humbled, and those who humble themselves will be exalted." This call to servitude is what we shall use to combat pride and feelings of self-conceit.

Now if we were servants by force, then our service would not mean much. God does not want to force us. He would rather us follow Christ's calling to service by choice. We must choose to be of use to others, putting others before ourselves. For example, in Luke 14:8–11, Christ tells us,

> When you are invited to a wedding feast, don't sit in the seat of honor. What if someone who is more distinguished than you has also been invited? The host will come and say, "Give this person your seat." Then you will be embarrassed, and you will have to take whatever seat is left at the foot of the table! Instead, take the lowest place at the foot of the table. Then when your host sees you, he will

come and say, "Friend, we have a better place for you!" Then you will be honored in front of all the other guests. For those who exalt themselves will be humbled, and those who humble themselves will be exalted.

Though we may not *feel* very humble all the time, we should still choose the humble path, for the more we do a thing, the easier it becomes, and soon it becomes a habit. I know this is the case for me. There was a time in my life when I would have rushed to be the first person in line, a time when I would have been unwilling to share certain things for fear that there would not be enough left over for me. These were the behaviors of a fearful, selfish, and prideful person. I was concerned with my own needs over the needs of others, and I assumed that I deserved my spot in line because I had the good sense to get there first. Many people feel this way. We do this without realizing why we do it. Now, however, through a relationship with Jesus Christ, I rarely struggle with this problem.

Now I often let others get in front of me in line, whether they ask to or not. I try to wait until the end to receive any goods or services, and I am usually helping others while I wait for the line to go down. I perform these actions out of habit. It does not even cross my mind to think about how I make sure everyone else has a seat before I take one for myself or find a place on the floor. This kind of service and humility comes to me naturally, and when I reflect on it, I feel noble and purposeful. Even though there is the risk that everything may be gone by the time I take my turn, God always provides for me, and the benefits of being humble far outweigh the drawbacks. Humility has become a habit, and anyone can pick it up.

Thinking about the welfare of others before oneself is a godlike action, and as we know, godlike behavior leads to joy. George Bernard Shaw says that life's true joy comes from "being used for a purpose recognized by yourself as a mighty one; the being thoroughly worn out before you are thrown on the scrap heap; the being a force of Nature instead of a feverish selfish little clod of ailments and grievances complaining that the world will not devote itself to making you happy."[1] Hard work in the service of your brothers and sisters has an intrinsic joy attached to it. I know it seems that the opposite might be true and that having *others serve you* would bring you happiness, but you must not be deceived, brothers and sisters. This is simply a trick of the enemy, and we were not meant to live in such a manner.

Christ came to serve, and he gives us the example for how to live on this earth. If Christ served, we must serve. It might not sound pleasant to you; however, it is a unique and wonderful experience, and it certainly has its rewards. Just as the wedding guest in the parable was honored after he humbled himself, our Lord finds all sorts of reasons to honor those who serve others. Our lives are full of blessings and favor. I believe that it is a result of both God's goodness and the servant's humility. Remember that the Pharisees desired the places of honor and special seats in the synagogue. If you do not want to become counted among them, you must practice humility.

Finally, if nothing else makes you want to be humble, remember Christ's words in Matthew 18:3–4, which says, "I tell you the truth, unless you turn from your sins and become like little children, you will never get into the Kingdom of Heaven. So anyone who becomes as humble as this little child is the greatest in the Kingdom of Heaven." Since we all want to enter the kingdom of heaven, we must take Jesus' advice and create the new habit of humble service. I recommend the book *Leader Shifts* by Joseph Warren Walker III, and I recommend the chapter "From Servant to Steward." This message will benefit all, especially those in leadership positions.

So why do you condemn another believer? Why do you look down on another believer? Remember, we will all stand before the judgment seat of God. For the Scriptures say, "'As surely as I live,' says the Lord, 'every knee will bend to me, and every tongue will declare allegiance to God.'" Yes, each of us will give a personal account to God. So let's stop condemning each other. Decide instead to live in such a way that you will not cause another believer to stumble and fall.

—Romans 14:10–13

Chapter 19

Now that we have established humility as a necessary character trait on our journey to being godlike, we can move on to seeking righteousness with the understanding that we should do it in a humble manner. God is right. In regards to righteousness for the Christian, we should remember that through a relationship with Christ, God makes us right. Though we will not be saved by righteousness, it is a necessary part of our Christian race, and it will bring us closer to God and thus closer to joy. What does righteousness look like? I am hesitant to give a description for fear that you will either say, "Of course I am all of those things," or, "That's impossible. No one could possibly be all of that." Rather it is easier to speak about what righteousness does not look like, and Paul does an excellent job of it in Ephesians 5:1–4.

> Imitate God, therefore, in everything you do, because you are his dear children. Live a life filled with love, following the example of Christ. He loved us and offered himself as a sacrifice for us, a pleasing aroma to God. Let there be no sexual immorality, impurity, or greed among you. Such sins have no place among God's people. Obscene stories, foolish talk, and coarse jokes—these are not for you. Instead, let there be thankfulness to God.

These worldly actions Paul has listed—sexual immorality, greed, foul talk, etc.—are all examples of things that are not right and thus not righteous. Unfortunately these actions are still a part of the lives of many Christians. When I was taking shots and drinking too much, I was guilty of doing all these worldly things. My talk was foul, I was promiscuous, and though I was not especially greedy, I was definitely behaving selfishly. In those times of worldliness, I was not in right standing with God, and I was not in good standing with my neighbor either. I couldn't be of any help to anyone who needed a relationship with Christ in my inebriated state. Oh sure, I could talk about how awesome God is, but I am sure such a speech loses its conviction when the speaker is slurring her words, has to take pauses to throw up, or is later caught making out in the corner.

This worldly behavior does not help make disciples as we are called to do. "Well, I am not hurting anyone when I tell a dirty story or a foul joke," you may say, but you have to remember your responsibilities as a Christian. You are always setting an example for others. Tadodaho Chief Leon Shenandoah believed that we are all teachers that every day we must behave responsibly and in the way that we would want others to mimic because we are constantly being watched. Others will behave the way they see us behave. If we do wrong, they will do wrong, but if we do right, they will do right as well. You know that certain things are wrong, and you would not want others to do them, so you shouldn't do them either. Whenever you commit an action, you are saying that this action is acceptable and that this behavior is something you support. Thus, make all your actions righteous so no one can point to you and say, "Well, she did it, or he did it." Choose righteousness at all times.[1]

Sometimes you should or shouldn't do certain things because of other people's feelings. Sometimes righteousness calls for doing what is right for others and not yourself. For example, though I no longer take shots, I still drink in moderation. I do not think that drinking is a sin as long as it is not excessive. But there are times when I am among people who believe that drinking is a sin, and when I am with these people, I do not drink, not because *I* believe it is wrong but because they do. Paul talks about this in his letter to the people of Corinth. Paul asks,

> Suppose someone tells you, "This meat was offered to an idol." Don't eat it, out of consideration for the conscience of the one who told you. It might not be a matter of conscience for you, but it is for the other person. For why should my freedom be limited by what someone else thinks? If I can thank God for the food and enjoy it, why should I be condemned for eating it? So whether you eat or drink, or whatever you do, do it all for the glory of God. Don't give offense to Jews or Gentiles or the church of God. I, too, try to please everyone in everything I do. I don't just do what is best for me; I do what is best for others so that many may be saved. (1 Corinthians 10:28–32)

When Paul eats among the Jews, they require a kosher meal. By this time he has been delivered from the burden of the law through a relationship with Christ, but he still eats kosher when he is with those who require it. He does not do what is best for him but what is best for others. This lesson can be applied to an abundance of scenarios in our lives. As Christians, we must be tuned in to the conditions of the people around us. We cannot focus merely on ourselves, but we must be conscious of the needs of others. In this way we can help bring people to Christ, or if they are already Christians, we can help them to stay in right standing with God through our good example.

As we look for things to fill ourselves up with now that we are emptying ourselves of worldly things, we can again look to

Christ for a wise example. Jesus speaks on the importance of righteousness many times. He tells us we must hunger and thirst after it, that we will be persecuted for it, that we will be convicted for it, and that we should seek after it (Matthew 5:6; 5:10: 6:33; John 16:8). Cleary it is important. He also talks about how our righteousness must exceed that of the scribes and Pharisees. Remember that they were trying to be righteous by following every letter of the law, but our righteousness comes in the form of love as was modeled by Jesus Christ.

In order to fill ourselves up with righteousness, we must think about what it means to love God and our neighbor in any given moment. Love is always the right action. Love is always the action that will make us godlike. I recommend you read *To Become a Human Being: The Message of Tadodaho Chief Leon Shenandoah* by Steve Wall. Though I do not agree with every word in the book, it offers a powerful take on what it means to be human and in relationship with both the Creator and other people. It is full of powerful teachings on how to live righteously, and it will be a blessing to any mature Christian who reads it with an open mind.

Trust in the Lord with all your heart; do not depend on your own understanding. Seek his will in all you do, and he will show you which path to take. Don't be impressed with your own wisdom. Instead, fear the Lord and turn away from evil. Then you will have healing for your body and strength for your bones.

—Proverbs 3:5–8

Chapter 20

The next habit we should cultivate in our lives is wisdom. Wisdom is a mighty tool in our battle against the enemy. In many ways it can help us combat one of the enemy's greatest tricks, temptation. When we are wise, we will be better able to make those decisions that will allow us to overcome temptation. Now I am not talking about wisdom in the worldly sense of being smart or acquiring knowledge over time. Wisdom for the Christian means trusting in God and the Holy Spirit to make the best decisions for our lives. Just as the quote from Proverbs says, we must trust in the Lord with all our hearts and not rely on our own knowledge and understanding of things. Thus, a great deal of wisdom comes from simply praying to God and letting go of our already limited power in a situation. For me wisdom often means not making impulsive decisions but taking the time to pray and waiting for a response from the Holy Spirit before I move forward.

True wisdom, even if it comes from knowledge gained over time, is always from above. Paul knew this fact and wrote to the people of Corinth, "Stop deceiving yourselves. If you think you are wise by this world's standards, you need to become a fool to be truly wise. For the wisdom of this world is foolishness to God. As the Scriptures say, 'He traps the wise in the snare of their own cleverness.' And again, 'The Lord knows the thoughts of the wise; he knows they are worthless'" (1 Corinthians 3:18–20). The problem for many of us lies in the fact that we already count ourselves wise because we went to school or study the Word.

Now both of these actions are awesome, and I highly recommend them; however, when compared with an all-knowing God of the universe, they still fall short of wisdom.

So how then do we acquire wisdom if we cannot gain it through study or experience? We obtain wisdom by asking for it from God in all the things that we do and at all moments of decision making no matter how small. The truly wise person knows that God cares about the minute and mundane details of our lives. When we come to see God as Father and look to God to supply all our needs just as a child relies on his or her parents, we become wise. We are wise and peaceful, and because we are not worried about anything, we are full of joy just as a small child is full of joy. What holds us back from peace and joy as adults are all the difficult decisions we have to make. These important decisions weigh us down with worry and stress. But when we develop the habit of wisdom, we can be freed from our burdens and experience joy. All we need to do is ask God. James 1:5–8 tells us,

> If you need wisdom, ask our generous God, and he will give it to you. He will not rebuke you for asking. But when you ask him, be sure that your faith is in God alone. Do not waver, for a person with divided loyalty is as unsettled as a wave of the sea that is blown and tossed by the wind. Such people should not expect to receive anything from the Lord. Their loyalty is divided between God and the world, and they are unstable in everything they do.

Simply by asking God and trusting the answer whenever there is a decision to make, we become wise.

Wisdom is an excellent trait to have, as it is a benefit in all of life's circumstances. The development of wisdom takes time. You must learn to trust God with all decisions, and you must also train yourself to go to God for even the smallest choices in your life. Most of us are so used to figuring things out on our own and being self-reliant that developing the habit of going to God for every little thing will be very difficult for us. Nonetheless, we must learn to rely on God if we are to achieve wisdom and joy.

In order to help you become reliant on God, I recommend taking time every morning to think about the previous day and look for times you could have gone to God to make a decision. Pray that this day you will do better and try to remember your prayer throughout the day. I recommend you read the book of Corinthians, which Paul wrote to the church in Corinth. Paul speaks a great deal on the topic of wisdom and how it relates to Christians. Use this to help guide you toward wisdom in your own life.

Then Jesus told them, "I tell you the truth, if you have faith and don't doubt, you can do things like this and much more. You can even say to this mountain, 'May you be lifted up and thrown into the sea,' and it will happen. You can pray for anything, and if you have faith, you will receive it."

—Matthew 21:21–22

Chapter 21

Walking hand in hand with wisdom is faith. If wisdom asks you to go to God for all decision making, faith demands that you trust in God in all actions, even those that are instinctive. Faith believes that every move is one that brings you closer to things hoped for and to things not seen. Faith is living your life in a way that trusts God to take care of an unknown future. When a child wakes in the morning, he or she wakes up carefree. The child is not immediately bombarded with the worries of the day. There are no bills to be anxious over, no coworkers to contend with, and no failing health to be concerned about. Average children wake up feeling carefree with the faith that their mothers and fathers are going to provide all their needs for the day. Unfortunately this is not true for every child, but it is for the majority. If the parents can be trusted, then the children can be happy and carefree with the knowledge that all their needs are cared for. This is what God wants for each and every one of us.

God wants us to be happy and carefree because we have faith in God to take care of everything in an unknown future. Hebrews 11:6 tells us, "It is impossible to please God without faith. Anyone who wants to come to him must believe that God exists and that he rewards those who sincerely seek him." God wants to be our Father, and just as a boy depends on his father to take care of everything, God wants us to depend on him. The world tries to convince us that we must be self-reliant and depend on no one but ourselves, and though this is true as it relates to the world, our relationship with God is quite different. We can depend on

God, and depending on God is required to live a life of joy. Søren Kierkegaard tells us, "Faith is convinced that God is concerned about the smallest things."[1] This means that no issue in our lives is too small for God. There is no aspect of our lives too minor or too obscure for God to be concerned about it. If we want to please God, we must depend on God even in the small things.

Now you might ask yourself, "What does this look like? What does a person of faith do so that you know they have faith? How can you tell?" James 2:14–18 tells us that we know a person has faith when we see them helping others. He says,

> What good is it, dear brothers and sisters, if you say you have faith but don't show it by your actions? Can that kind of faith save anyone? Suppose you see a brother or sister who has no food or clothing, and you say, "Good-bye and have a good day; stay warm and eat well"—but then you don't give that person any food or clothing. What good does that do? So you see, faith by itself isn't enough. Unless it produces good deeds, it is dead and useless. Now someone may argue, "Some people have faith; others have good deeds." But I say, "How can you show me your faith if you don't have good deeds? I will show you my faith by my good deeds."

This passage by James makes it clear that we know people of faith when we see them helping others. But the following question still remains: How does doing good works prove you have faith? Doing good works and helping others proves you have faith because the natural order of the world would have you look out for yourselves only. It makes no sense to give resources to other people because you might one day need them for yourself. But what about your instinct to be a part of a community because there is safety in numbers? Yes, this is an instinct, but this instinct is also an act of faith. You give to members of the community in the hopes that they may be there for you if you are ever in need. You are still stepping out on things hoped for, so it is still an act of faith. The difference concerns what you are putting your faith in.

Are you putting your faith in God or in other people? If you answered yes to the latter, I am afraid you are making a grave mistake. People will let you down, as we are all flawed sinners. Thus, we come back to the truth of doing good as an act of faith in God. When you help others, you are saying that you trust that God will be there to help and provide for you when it is your turn for help. God may very well use other people to provide that help, but never doubt that God is the source from which all your help comes. By sharing your resources, you are saying to the helped person that there is a good and powerful God out there who will provide all our needs and that I have enough to share with you. In contrast to what the dictionary may say, faith is a verb. It is an act of stepping out. Faith is knowing and living like you know everything is going to be all right because the Lord of the universe has control and cares for every aspect of your life. Now that we understand what faith is and why we need to develop it as a habit, we must talk about how to gain faith.

The Bible is very clear on this point. "Faith comes by hearing and hearing by the word of God" (Romans 10:17 KJV). We must constantly hear words of faith. We can do this in several ways. A few of them include participating in personal and corporate prayer, reading the Bible, listening to spiritual music, reading biblical literature, and of course, attending a worship service. Faith is like a car in that it runs on fuel. It must be constantly fueled up on the Word of God. When you go too long without filling up, your faith will suffer. You must build the habit of taking in the Word of God regularly. The more you hear the Word, the better your faith and the closer you will be to joy. I recommend reading Søren Kierkegaard's *Fear and Trembling*. It speaks in great length on faith and how unique and awesome it is.

I am convinced that God is love; for me the thought has a primal lyrical validity. When it is present to me, I am unspeakably happy; when it is absent, I long for it more vehemently than the lover for the object of his love.[1]

—Søren Kierkegaard

Chapter 22

The next habit or behavior we need to acquire is love. Love is extremely important for us as Christians. Christ tells us that the two greatest commandments are to love God with all that you are and to love your neighbor in the same way that you love yourself. All the other behaviors we have discussed up until now will come to us more naturally when we learn to love in these two ways. What then is love? Like faith, love can be difficult to recognize. Erich Fromm, a renowned psychologist, wrote a book titled *The Art of Loving*. In his book he gives a definition of love. He believes that love is active. Loving is the act of working for the thing or person we love. It is a verb and is always manifest in the act of showing concern. Thus, we can judge the love we have for someone or something by the care with which we attend to the person or thing. For example, most mothers labor at cooking and cleaning for their children out of their loving concern for the child's well-being. Fathers too labor at jobs to provide homes and food for their children. Parents show their love by laboring to care and provide for their children.[2]

When people love a job, a car, or a pet, it is no different. You can tell that they love it by the work they put into caring for it. The same should be true for our relationship with God. We can know if we love God by how much time we are willing to spend seeking God's face. When we love God, we are actively concerned about the growth of our relationship with God. We labor at getting closer to God and knowing God better because we know that this brings God pleasure and that it is in our own best interest.

When we grow our ability to love, we become more godlike. Just as God is love, we must also become love if we want to be godlike.

Because love is godlike, we know that love is a powerful tool to be used against the enemy. It was used as such a tool by two great men named Mahatma Gandhi and Martin Luther King Jr. These two men used the power of love and nonviolent resistance to end tyranny and racial injustice for their people. As an option over selfishness, indifference, and hate, love is one of the few weapons we possess to use against the evils in our world. Love works to conquer evil because it is a universal truth. The truth is that all people desire love. Everyone in the world wants to be loved no matter who they are. The problem is that so many of us have experienced rejection or pain associated with love, and because of this pain, our ability to love is defiled. Because of this defiled form of love, which many of us suffer from, we act in hate and hurt each other in an attempt to make ourselves feel better. In turn, the person or people we are hurting react with hate to our hate, and the cycle keeps going. If we choose, however, to react to one another's hate with love, we are more likely to break the cycle with time.

Martin Luther King Jr. explains how love is able to break the cycle of hate in his essay titled "My Trip to the Land of Gandhi." King says that nonviolent resistance is not a cowardly and powerless act as some people believe. Rather it is a courageous act based on a revelation that the lover has experienced. The revelation is that violence only begets violence, but loving someone who is behaving violently toward you can cause shame in them. If you can get the person to feel ashamed of themselves, then there is a good possibility that the person will change and stop his or her acts of hatred. King and Gandhi were each able to enact great change by choosing to love their enemies rather than hate them. Even when you are being treated badly by others, you still have the ability to choose love and righteousness. You are not obligated to react with violence to violence. King shows us that by choosing to love our enemies as the Bible says we should, we have a chance to transform and bring a change of heart. God can use our love toward our enemies to shame them into change, but if our actions are evil in return, there is no opportunity for shame.[3]

Love then is important for multiple reasons. It is necessary for making disciples, for having a relationship with God, who is love, and finally for having peace in one's own soul. In Dr. King's speech "Where Do We Go from Here?" he speaks eloquently on the effects of love on our human condition. He talks about how violence can only cause more violence and says that this is not something he wants for himself. He speaks of how he saw hatred on the faces of his oppressors in the South. Hatred like that changes a person. It taints the soul and permeates every aspect of life. King did not want this for himself. Instead of reacting with hate, he choose to love no matter how others behaved toward him—if for no other reason than to keep his spirit free from the weight of hatred. Brothers and sisters, we must remove all hate from our lives and instead choose love. We must do it not just for those around us but for ourselves. Hate is a trick of the enemy, and it will only lead to our destruction. No matter what has happened, no matter what you have been through, know that only love can heal you. Holding on to hate will poison you, and your joy will only come with love.[4]

So my brothers and sisters, I call for you to love. Love God because God first loved you. Love your neighbor because God choose to love you even through your many mistakes and imperfections. Love your neighbor because love is the only power that can extinguish hate. The Bible says that vengeance is the Lord's and that we are not to repay evil for evil. If you want to have joy, you cannot be the cause of suffering in another person. No matter what someone has done to you, you still have a choice over how you will react. Hating them will not help them get better. Only love can. I recommend you read the gospel of John.

Read about God's great love for the world in sending his only begotten Son. Know through this gospel that love is God's divine plan for all of our lives, and choose love because it is inherent to your human nature and a vital step on your journey toward joy.

Most of the luxuries, and many of the so called comforts of life, are not only not indispensable, but positive hindrances to the elevation of mankind.[1]

—Henry David Thoreau

A man is rich in proportion to the number of things which he can afford to let alone.[2]

—Henry David Thoreau

Chapter 23

In the final chapter on habits, we will cover the issue of self-control, one of the things most every person lacks to some degree. We all want self-control and know we need it, but it is not easily obtained. For me it is a constant struggle. Like Paul, I do those things I don't want to do, and I do not do what I want to do. I know what is good and what is right, but I let my own sinful nature and the words of the enemy team up to override what I know in my heart to be correct. Having self-control is a constant daily struggle that we all fight. We wage war within ourselves over little things like whether or not to have that second piece of cake, whether to go bed at your bedtime or stay up late to watch a show, or whether to have just one more drink before you cut yourself off. We are all struggling with temperance, which is having just enough and then stopping or doing enough and not being lazy to the task. If we want to be more temperate, we must come to the knowledge that temperance and self-control are gifts from the Holy Spirit.

When Paul lays out the works of the flesh and the fruit of the Spirit to the church in Galatia, he mentions most all of the habits we have been speaking about. He states that "the Holy Spirit produces this kind of fruit in our lives: love, joy, peace, patience, kindness, goodness, faithfulness, gentleness, and self-control. There is no law against these things!" (Galatians 5:22–23). From Christ we know the most important of these fruits to be love, but if I had to pick a number two, I would choose self-control. Self-control is precious because it is so close and yet so elusive. It is close because it requires no outside help. No one can give you self-control, and your self-control has nothing to do with directing someone else. It is completely consumed with the self. The whole purpose of this book is for us to learn to better control ourselves and move ourselves toward joy. As simple as self-control seems, it is elusive. Self-control is something you could very well struggle with your entire life.

Controlling our own actions and choices at all times is a mighty task and not easily accomplished. God has luckily given us all we need to achieve success. In 2 Peter's 1:3–8, he makes it clear that we have everything that we need to experience self-control. Peter says of God,

> By his divine power, God has given us everything we need for living a godly life. We have received all of this by coming to know him, the one who called us to himself by means of his marvelous glory and excellence. And because of his glory and excellence, he has given us great and precious promises. These are the promises that enable you to share his divine nature and escape the world's corruption caused by human desires. In view of all this, make every effort to respond to God's promises. Supplement your faith with a generous provision of moral excellence, and moral excellence with knowledge, and knowledge with self-control, and self-control with patient endurance, and patient endurance with godliness, and godliness with brotherly affection, and brotherly affection with love for everyone. The more you grow like this, the more productive and useful you will be in your knowledge of our Lord Jesus Christ.

In the beginning of this passage, Peter tells us that God has granted us everything that has to do with life and godliness. We access this knowledge through the knowledge of Christ, who called us to follow him in glory and excellence. The prize for following Christ in excellence is the ability to partake of the divine nature or godliness. This is good news since we have established that we must be godlike in order to have joy. The caveat is that we must also deny or be set apart from the sinful and corrupt world, which means we must have self-control.

When we empty ourselves of worldly things, we must fill ourselves back up with self-control. We must train ourselves to love self-denial and discipline. This sounds difficult, but truly when you come to understand the nature of humanity, you see that this is actually a natural calling and embedded in the DNA of all mankind. Kierkegaard talks about self-denial in terms of resignation. He talks about how we must resign from the world in order to take control of the self. Kierkegaard states that resignation from the world is a high calling and that if we choose not to do it, it is because we are cowards. When we resign from the world, we become our own censors, and in doing so, we take a leap of faith that brings us ever closer to God. Resignation from the world is necessary in order to reconcile your soul to God. To access the joy that comes as a side effect of godliness, there must be a resignation from the world, and this resignation requires self-control.[3] We must remove ourselves as part of the world in order to properly follow Christ. Paul called it crucifying the flesh daily. Denying ourselves and seeking God is what we are here to do. As Paul says to the Athenians in Acts 17:27–28, "His purpose was for the nations to seek after God and perhaps feel their way toward him and find him—though he is not far from any one of us. For in him we live and move and exist. As some of your own poets have said, 'We are his offspring.'" Self-denial is truly one of the greatest gifts we can give ourselves because when we lose our sinful natures as a part of the corrupt world, we position ourselves to gain eternity.

I hope that I have convinced you of the benefits of self-control and self-denial. If I have and you wish to achieve self-control, the first thing you must do is pray, for self-control is a gift from God. As Paul tells us in 2 Timothy 1:7, "God has not given us a spirit of fear and timidity, but of power, love, and self-discipline." Thus, if we are going to accomplish self-control, we must seek the help of our heavenly Father. Secondly you must meditate on the idea of denying the world. Spend time thinking about what this means for you as an individual and what your worldly pulls are. Remember that you must give up the corrupt world in order to embrace Christ and find joy and peace. Don't forget that the world is run by the enemy and that the worldly things that you are cleaving to may give you momentary happiness but at the expense of a lasting joy and peace.

Thirdly you must forgive yourself. You are not perfect, and your attempts at self-denial and control will not work out the first time or the fifth time. This is a long road, and it will take a great deal of time to travel it. You must not let a setback hold you back from trying again. Remember that God is love and your heavenly Father does not condemn you for making mistakes. He believes in you every time you get back up to try again. The enemy is the one who tries to tell you it is hopeless. Don't believe him. Finally I recommend reading *Walden* by Henry David Thoreau. Thoreau goes out into the woods to live on purpose. He resigns himself from the world in order to get to the truth of life. His self-control and self-denial are admirable, and there is a lot to be learned from what he experienced.

There is much more we would like to say about this, but it is difficult to explain, especially since you are spiritually dull and don't seem to listen. You have been believers so long now that you ought to be teaching others. Instead, you need someone to teach you again the basic things about God's word. You are like babies who need milk and cannot eat solid food. For someone who lives on milk is still an infant and doesn't know how to do what is right. Solid food is for those who are mature, who through training have the skill to recognize the difference between right and wrong.

—Hebrews 5:11–14

Chapter 24

We made it. We have come to the end of our work. We have said quite a bit about the nature of joy and what it means to be godlike. If you can remember back to our first chapter, we discussed how Aristotle believed that we receive joy by having virtuous characters. We have debated numerous habits that we either want to cultivate or remove from our lives in order to obtain virtuous characters. We have concluded that if we commit to a life of virtue, discipline, and discipleship, we are sure to achieve the joy promised to us by God.

This chapter, the second to the last, is different from the previous chapters. This chapter acknowledges the skeptics. I want to address those who have read this work and are thinking one of these two things: One, it cannot be done. This person may have been a Christian for years and still has not achieved virtue or joy. Nor has anyone else they know. It is all well and good to talk about achieving joy, but while we are on earth, it is just not practical. These are the people I will call defeatist. The second group of skeptics wonders why they have to work so hard and be so disciplined at all. Why were we not born perfect? Why would a perfect God create imperfect beings? I like to call these people the philosopher Christians. If you are in either of these two groups, do not worry. I do not condemn you, and I know God certainly does not. I will attempt to put both of these arguments to rest in this chapter. First I will deal with the later skeptic, the philosopher.

The philosopher's question boils down to the following: Why do we have free will? Why is it that we are free to sin when sin is wrong and God doesn't want us to do wrong? Well, philosopher, there is a very good reason for free will, and C. S. Lewis does an excellent job explaining it. Lewis states that we need free will because without it we would all be robots. A world made up of robots—even though they would keep evil from happening—keeps love from happening. The ability to do evil gets a world that also gives people the ability to love.

Lewis goes on to explain that with freedom comes choice. You can choose to do right, or you can choose to do wrong. The two work as a team. Without the other, neither of them would exist. We would not know or appreciate good without the presence and knowledge of bad. "Well, that is no great loss," you may say. "It is okay to lose good as long as bad is gone." But think about all your favorite things—your favorite food, activities, or TV shows. Does not the distinction between good and bad make these things your favorite? And without a distinction of likes and dislikes, what is it that makes you … you? How would you define yourself without these judgment calls? You wouldn't be able to. Instead, we would all be identical. Again, we would all be robots.[1]

God knows that living, loving, thinking beings are much better than robots. Robots cannot love you. Robots simply fulfill their tasks, and as much as you may appreciate them, they will never love you back. So God did not make us robots. No, we are sinful creatures that have the ability to overcome our sinful natures, and through God's grace, we can be made virtuous. When we learn to get past our simplistic and human ideas of God, we can embrace the glorious free will God has given us with the knowledge that we choose virtue and righteousness. No one forces our hand. The choice is what makes virtue significant and worthy. Choosing to do something rather than being forced is admirable in all walks of life. It is the struggle and the effort we put into something that makes us admire and appreciate one another. We all appreciate those who are passionate and work hard at their craft no matter what it is.

If an athlete is naturally talented, that is all well and good, but if he or she never worked at it, if he or she never had to practice or struggle, we would appreciate his or her talent but not his or her character. Those things that come easy to us are regarded with little value. But when there are obstacles to overcome, or when the athlete is dedicated and always training at his or her craft, we as a society appreciate the athlete's character. It is the same with virtue. If we were all naturally virtuous and without sin, then there would be no glory in it. But because we are not, the glory lies in the fact that we must struggle and perfect our craft of virtue and godliness. That is why we have free will and are not perfect beings.

Now let's move to the defeatist skeptic. This person believes that virtue cannot be obtained and that our sinful natures are too strong for us to overcome here on earth. First I must tell you that this thought did not come from God. God believes in you and is supportive of you, and this defeatist thought comes not from God but from the enemy. The enemy is telling you that it is too hard and that it cannot be done. He tells you this because he wants you to be defeated by sin. He wants you to forget that Christ gave you the victory over sin. If he can convince you to not even try to be virtuous, then he has succeeded in stealing your joy. The enemy wants to convince you that you cannot also have joy if you have earthly trials and that you can only have joy in your life if your life is perfect. If you are to fight the enemy on this point, you must do it through faith and the knowledge that the enemy is lying. You can still have joy if you have trials. We have learned through this work that the joy that comes from having a virtuous character as a gift from God works regardless of the trials you are currently experiencing. The happenings of life are irrelevant to our joy because our joy comes from a relationship with God, a being that is not of the earth.

When God allowed the Devil to plague the life of Job, his *friends* tried to convince him that it was his fault he was experiencing these catastrophes and that he had done something wrong to cause it. But Job confidently argued with them that he was blameless, and in the end God reveals that he was right. When you choose virtue, you may still have trials; however, that does not necessarily mean it is your fault, and it certainly does not mean that you cannot also have joy. If you want to be godlike and virtuous, you must work at it, and you must believe that it is possible. How do you work at it? We do so through prayer, study, meditation, and hearing the Word of God spoken over our lives. We must constantly fill our lives with the things of God. Not a day should go by when we do not pray, read our Bibles, or talk to God. We must work diligently toward our goal. We must also constantly remind ourselves of what our goal is so that we do not lose sight of it.

Finally I encourage you with this quote from Peter 1:2–3which says, "So get rid of all evil behavior. Be done with all deceit, hypocrisy, jealousy, and all unkind speech. Like newborn babies, you must crave pure spiritual milk so that you will grow into a full experience of salvation. Cry out for this nourishment, now that you have had a taste of the Lord's kindness." I recommend you read *What Christians Believe* by C. S. Lewis. You can specifically review the chapter titled "The Shocking Alternative," which speaks a great deal on free will and why it is important.

What God cares about is not exactly our actions. What he cares about is that we should be creatures of a certain kind or quality—the kind of creatures he intended us to be—creatures related to himself in a certain way.[1]

—C. S. Lewis

Chapter 25

After all that we have discussed—and it was only a small portion of what could be said—you should now be able to step away from this work with a plan. If you have not been taking notes and writing out inspirational quotes as I suggested in the beginning, please reread the book and do so. Now it is time to create your battle plan. Write out the program that will help you resist temptation, build up your faith, and draw closer to God daily and in all that you do. In this final chapter, I want to paint a picture of what a disciple of Christ look like. I will attempt to describe the typical day for a disciple of Christ, living in enemy-occupied territory, trying to grow closer to God each day, and living out his or her God-given purpose.

The day begins early, not that it must begin at a certain hour of the day. It starts long before disciples are required to be at work or at school. It begins early because disciples do not want to be rushed and hurried. They want the time to do things decently and do them in order. Disciples begin their day in prayer and devotion. They go to God on their knees in their closets and thank God for waking them up another day. They ask their Savior to help them die to the things of the flesh that day because they know they are sinners. In order to be disciples, we must hate our sinful natures. As it says in Luke 14:26–27, "If you want to be my disciple, you must hate everyone else by comparison—your father and mother, wife and children, brothers and sisters—yes, even your own life. Otherwise, you cannot be my disciple. And if you do not carry your own cross and follow me, you cannot be my disciple." Thus, disciples ask to have their flesh crucified daily so that they can be fruitful and useful to the Lord Jesus Christ.

After prayers, there is a period of religious reading during which time the Lord may send a message through the Word. Once the time of prayer and devotion is over, disciples begin their day just like any other person would. However, on the way to work or school, they choose to listen to the Word of God so that their faith will be built up. They do not listen to secular music or talk radio but rather listen to gospel music or religious oratory so that they may be filled with the Word before they go out into the world. If they do have a family, they will engage their family in productive conversation and speak life over them so that their children and spouses will also be filled and protected throughout their day. They work hard at their jobs, knowing that the work they do is a reflection of God and should glorify the Lord. Throughout their day disciples are speaking words of life over those around them and are making morally mature decisions. If others are speaking words of negativity, disciples are very intentional about avoiding such conversations. If they cannot avoid them, they diffuse them by boldly standing on the Word of God and proclaiming God's greatness over every area of life in the hopes that they may elicit a change in their peers through their own good influence.

After formal work, disciples go home and fill their leisure time with activities that glorify God. They may attend Bible study, watch religious movies, engage in religious readings, or simply spend quality time with their spouses and children. Regardless of what they do, they keep God with them and try to do things in an honest and moral way. They follow the teachings of Paul in Colossians 3:9–11, which reads, "Don't lie to each other, for you have stripped off your old sinful nature and all its wicked deeds. Put on your new nature, and be renewed as you learn to know your Creator and become like him. In this new life, it doesn't matter if you are a Jew or a Gentile, circumcised or uncircumcised, barbaric, uncivilized, slave, or free. Christ is all that matters, and he lives in all of us."

As the day winds down, they continue to work diligently and steadily so that they are not rushed but are living out the purpose that God has given them. Before they go to bed, it is again time for prayers. They thank God for another good day. They admit their mistakes from the day, and they ask God to help them work on those areas that need improvement. They commit to running their race again the next day if God sees fit to give them one more chance, but if not, they commit their spirits to God's hands. They pray for their family, friends, and people of concern. Finally they crawl into bed, tired from the day's diligent work, and they sleep, God willing, for the exact number of hours it will take for them to wake early the next morning, rested and ready to start all over again. This is what a day in the life of a disciple typically looks like. It is a normal day for most people in the sense that disciples go to work, have leisure time, and go to bed just like everyone else. The difference comes in the daily prayers, devotional reading, and commitment to righteousness. It does not mean that they made no mistakes that day. In this new life, you will make mistakes. You will not become flawless overnight, but you need not let your mistakes break the connection between you and God.

When we come to God in spirit and in truth, we are new beings living new lives. We are on a separate plane of existence than those who have not accepted Christ. We know this because Paul tells us in 2 Corinthians 5:16–17, "So we have stopped evaluating others from a human point of view. At one time we thought of Christ merely from a human point of view. How differently we know him now! This means that anyone who belongs to Christ has become a new person. The old life is gone; a new life has begun!" At this level we know that all sin is truly sin against God, so when we repent, we repent to God and commit to doing better tomorrow. The true sin for us in this new life would be giving up on our race, throwing in the towel, and no longer even trying to be virtuous and Christlike. This is the worst thing we can do. Part of this new life includes developing those habits that will make us virtuous and godlike and removing those habits that keep us worldly and separate us from God. We must separate ourselves from those things that tempt us by learning wisdom. When we are wise, we go to God and listen to the Holy Spirit in all situations and through every temptation. We know that no problem is too small for God and that diligent prayer helps us to avoid those situations we know hold temptation for us.

We must also break the habit of relying on money for security. We must remember that God is our provider, not our jobs or our bank accounts. We know that God gave us all we have, and it can all be easily taken away. Thus, we must place our faith and trust in God and not in money. Faith in God will never let us down and will free us from the sin that comes with the love of money. We must also be humble. We must know that self-importance and looking down on others is sinful. Furthermore, it is just plain foolish, for it is only by the grace of God that we are in the wonderful positions we are in. All our skills, promotions, and righteousness came from God, not from us. We could not have achieved any of our *great accomplishments* on our own. So it makes no sense to lord our given attributes over others. Rather we should follow the example of Christ by being humble and serving others. We know that even though Christ is far greater than any human is, ever was, or ever will be, he still washed the feet of his disciples and endured the shame of the cross for our sake.

We must also watch our words because we know that the power of life and death resides in the tongue. The words we speak over ourselves and others have significant effects and should not be taken lightly. In order to control our tongues, we must remember that our relationship with God is the most important thing in all the world and that God requires righteousness of us. But we cannot be made right when we speak all kinds of negativity over ourselves and others, for our own negative words will combat the righteousness God is trying to bestow on us. Thus, we must make righteousness a priority by working daily to speak life and not death and to live virtuously. We must also avoid arguments and anger by choosing to love and understand, for we know that anger and arguing rarely help a situation and only tend to make it worse. Instead, we must choose love for our neighbor because God first loved us, even though we are not perfect and are constantly falling short of the mark. So rather than become angry with our neighbors, we must love them in the knowledge that our love may produce a sense of shame in them and possibly bring about a change. We must hate every trace of the sin while we still love the sinner as a child of God.

Finally we must separate ourselves from all the worldly things that separate us from God. We do this by developing self-control and denying ourselves the things we know are not godly. Self-control will give us the ability to create good habits, remove bad ones, and become more godlike. Self-control, as we have recently learned, is one of the few things that we truly have control over. We cannot control others. We cannot control what crises befall us in life, but we can control how we react to things. If we were to lose everything and everyone we have in life just like Job did, we could still choose to trust God and give God glory no matter what was going on around us. Self-control is necessary in order to get to this place of trust and knowledge in God.

You must take this race toward joy seriously and make it a priority. You will not have joy until you dedicate yourself to the pursuit of godliness. Virtue and godliness have to become your life's purpose. You must pursue them with all that you have. The more you do this, the closer you will grow to God. Eventually you will be in a place of constant communion and symmetry with God. When this happens, you will have joy. When we pursue God with all that we are, we establish the kingdom of God on earth through our godly actions. In the kingdom there is no worry, anxiety, hate, malice, sickness, or sin. Rather there is joy, love, and kindness. I like what C. S. Lewis says about this transformation. At first Christianity seems all about right and wrong, good and evil, and following the rules. But it does not stay that way. Eventually the Christian moves past all that. Of course, doing right and avoiding wrong is a part of living as a Christian, but overtime it becomes less about that and more about having a relationship with the Lord, who is a marvel to behold. The better you get to know his ways, the more in awe you become. God is the great example of what it means to *be*. If we want to be anything, we should look to the Lord for our example. If you want to know what a disciple looks like, look at Christ. Jesus of Nazareth gives us the only recipe for true joy. He came to earth to die for our sins so that we might have life and have it more abundantly.[2]

I wrote this work to give myself more clarity on what I believe and what I must do to obtain joy. The Lord has revealed so much to me in the writing of this that I feel both humbled and overwhelmed. I hope that you will take something away from it, but if you remember only one thing, let it be that Christ has the recipe for your joy. Read the gospels, and when you are done, read them again and again. Meditate on the words of Christ, and I guarantee that you will see a change in your character. Be blessed, dear reader, in your pursuit of joy, and one day we will praise the Lord together forever. Amen.

Endnotes

Biblical quotes taken from: New Living Translation (NLT)

Holy Bible. New Living Translation copyright© 1996, 2004, 2007, 2013 by Tyndale House Foundation.

Chapter 1

[1] Henry Dyke, *The Van Dyke Book: Selected from the Writings of Henry Van Dyke* (New York: C. Scribner's Sons, 1905), xi.

[2] Justin D. Kaplan, ed., *The Pocket Aristotle*, trans. W. D. Ross (New York: Pocket Books, 1958), 173.

[3] 182.

Chapter 2

[1] Richard Warren, *The Purpose-Driven Life: What on Earth Am I Here For?* (Grand Rapids, MI: Zondervan, 2012), 36.

[2] Joel Osteen and Victoria Osteen, *Hope for Today Bible* (New YorkF: Free Press, 2009), 1390.

[3] G. M. A. Grube, *Five Dialogues*, Rev. John M. Cooper. II. (Indianapolis: Hackett Pub. Co., 2002), 40.

[4] Grube, G. M. A. *Five Dialogues*, 43.

Chapter 3

[1] Viktor E Frankl, *Man's Search for Meaning* (New York: Pocket Books, 1984), 136.

Chapter 4

[1] Howard C. Cutler, *The Art of Happiness: A Handbook for Living* (New York: Riverhead Books, 1998), 211.

Chapter 5

[1] Joel Osteen and Victoria Osteen, *Hope for Today Bible*,

[2] C. S. Lewis, *Mere Christianity* (San Francisco: Harper San Francisco, 2001), 87.

Chapter 6

1   Viktor E Frankl, *Man's Search for Meaning*, 99.
2   C. S. Lewis, *Mere Christianity*, 198.

Chapter 7

1   Ralph Waldo Emerson, Joel Porte, and Saundra Morris, *Emerson's Prose and Poetry: Authoritative Texts, Contexts, Criticism* (New York: W. W. Norton, 2001), 27.
2   Joel Osteen, *Your Best Life Now: 7 Steps to Living at Your Full Potential* (New York: Warner Books, 2004), 281.
3   Leon Shenandoah and Steve Wall, *To Become a Human Being: The Message of Tadodaho Chief Leon Shenandoah* (Charlottesville, VA: Hampton Roads Pub. Co., 2001), 87.

Chapter 8

1   Howard C. Cutler, *The Art of Happiness: A Handbook for Living*, 179.

Chapter 9

1   Nina Baym and Mary Loeffelholz, *Norton Anthology of American Literature*, 7th ed. (New York: W. W. Norton & Co., 2007), 266–267.
2   C. S. Lewis, *Mere Christianity*, 190–191.

Chapter 10

1   John Gneisenau Neihardt, *Black Elk Speaks: Being the Life Story of a Holy Man of the Oglala Sioux* (Lincoln: University of Nebraska Press, 1932), 33.

Chapter 12

1   C. S. Lewis, *The Weight of Glory* (London: Society for Promoting Christian Knowledge, 1942), 46.

Chapter 17

1   Armand M. Nicholi, *The Question of God: C. S. Lewis and Sigmund Freud Debate God, Love, Sex, and the Meaning of Life* (New York: Free Press, 2002), 122.
2   Blaise Pascal, *Pensées*, trans. A. J. Krailsheimer (London: Penguin Books, 1995), 57.

Chapter 19

1   Leon Shenandoah and Steve Wall. *To Become a Human Being: The Message of Tadodaho Chief Leon Shenandoah*, 44.

Chapter 21

1   Søren Kierkegaard, *Fear and Trembling/Repetition*. Howard V. Hong, and Edna H. Hong. (Princeton: Princeton University Press, 1983), 34.

Chapter 22

1   Søren Kierkegaard, *Fear and Trembling/Repetition*. Howard V. Hong, and Edna H. Hong., 34.

2   Erich Fromm, *The Art of Loving*, 1st ed. (New York: Harper & Row, 1956), 25–26.

3   Martin Luther King and James Melvin Washington, *I Have a Dream: Writings and Speeches that Changed the World* (San Francisco: Harper, 1992), 44.

4   Martin Luther King and James Melvin Washington, *I Have a Dream: Writings and Speeches that Changed the World*, 176.

Chapter 23

1   Nina Baym and Mary Loeffelholz, *Norton Anthology of American Literature*, 1814.

2   Nina Baym and Mary Loeffelholz, *Norton Anthology of American Literature*, 1850.

3   Søren Kierkegaard, *Fear and Trembling/Repetition*. Howard V. Hong, and Edna H. Hong., 48-49.

Chapter 24

1   Armand M. Nicholi, *The Question of God: C. S. Lewis and Sigmund Freud Debate God, Love, Sex, and the Meaning of Life*, 104.

Chapter 25

1   C. S. Lewis, *Mere Christianity*, 145.

2   C. S. Lewis, *Mere Christianity*, 149–150.

Printed in the United States
By Bookmasters